D1310100

# Pounce

Also by Ken Stern

*To Hell and Back*

*Secrets of the Investment All-Stars*

*Senior Savvy*

*50 Fabulous Places to Retire in America*

*Safeguard Your Hard-Earned Savings*

*The Comprehensive Guide
to Social Security and Medicare*

# Pounce

How to Seize Profit in
Today's Chaotic Markets

# Ken Stern

ST. MARTIN'S PRESS NEW YORK

The goal of this book is to offer information to the reader about the stock market. Investment strategies and theories cannot be guaranteed, and this book is sold with the understanding that neither the publisher nor the author is engaged in rendering professional services or in providing specific investment advice. Readers should consult with professional advisers and should choose investments that correspond to their financial needs, goals, and risk tolerance.

POUNCE. Copyright © 2009 by Ken Stern. All rights reserved.
Printed in the United States of America.
For information, address St. Martin's Press,
175 Fifth Avenue, New York, N.Y. 10010.

www.stmartins.com

Permission for figures on pages 50, 88, 128, and 160
© Copyright 2008 Ned Davis Research, Inc. Further distribution
prohibited without prior permission. All Rights Reserved.
See NDR Disclaimer at www.ndr.com/copyright.html.
For data vendor disclaimers refer to www.ndr.com/vendorinfo/.

Library of Congress Cataloging-in-Publication Data

Stern, Ken, 1965–
    Pounce : how to seize profit in today's chaotic markets / Ken
Stern.—1st ed.
        p. cm.
    ISBN-13: 978-0-312-55106-3
    ISBN-10: 0-312-55106-1
        1. Investments. 2 Stock exchanges. 3. Finance, Personal.
HG4515 .S75  2009
332.6—dc22
                                        2008043927

First Edition: March 2009

1   3   5   7   9   10   8   6   4   2

# CONTENTS

**Book Three: POUNCE**
The Personal Pounce Platform

# Pounce

# INTRODUCTION

Are you ready for a unique and exciting ride? Climb aboard and hold on tight! *Pounce* will begin to make you more aware of, and smarter about, superior investing and amassing serious wealth. But more than just making you aware, and unlike almost any other lesson you have enjoyed, this book will identify why you may have been or are encountering a ceiling preventing you from making more lucrative investments. Most importantly, even though you may not now possess skills in analysis, you will learn and execute a system designed to provide superior investment results—not in spite of adverse conditions but because of them. As effective as these systems are, you will not be active in managing your money more than once a month. You will formulate a monthly Pounce agenda. You'll adhere to this agenda. You'll Pounce.

This book will provide you with:

✓ The tools and strategies necessary to make educated investment decisions

- ✓ The skills you need in order to sort through information and obtain only what is critical
- ✓ A clearer understanding of markets, economies, and investing
- ✓ A system and a model that, if followed correctly, will enable you to build a well-developed wealth plan designed to take advantage of the chaos and extremes created in our daily life

## WHAT AND WHY?

I live by What and Why. What is Pounce, and why did I create it? Pounce is the only system that enables an investor to pinpoint specifically what is important to investment success. It shows you how to gather the tools needed to predispose you to success, and provides the strategy necessary to execute the plan. The best part is, I believe the easier you make a system, the easier success will be to achieve. People complicate things. People make complicated derivative and credit swaps. People create credit crises. People outsmart themselves. In fact, everything that Pounce is and represents can be summarized in three easy steps. Prior to the first step, as you will soon see, you must realize that part of why investment success is so elusive is because we rely too much on intuition and instinct. The underlying current through *Pounce* is to create and then trust in your systems, not let your emotions or your intuition complicate things.

### Step One
Follow the indicators that show you where the herd is going, and what to do about it.

**Step Two**

Learn how and when to Pounce on the investment strategies in Book Three. From Rising Stars to Pounce for Income and Growth, you will be provided with a specific screening process and instructed on exactly how and when to use each of these investment strategies.

**Step Three**

Create your Personal Pounce Platform (PPP). It gives you an answer and a discipline for every market, every situation, and, one hopes, a profitable pounce. And guess what? This is the best part: You are allowed to trade only once per month. Pounce is not a trading system. It is a wonderful investment strategy.

Most people, even analysts, invest based on intuition. Oh, sure, they do their research and tell you, based on their research, that they *believe* a stock is cheap. Or that they *believe* the market will go higher. Or that they *believe* a stock is fully valued and that it is time to sell. Then we learn that all of their research failed and the exact opposite occurred.

## YOUR DIAGNOSIS

I'm going to give it to you straight. I have read your chart, studied your brain, tested your IQ, and reviewed your lifestyle and investment history. The good news is you have the potential to realize great wealth through a great investing strategy. However, your brain exhibited dangerous readings. Your brain is actually predisposed to hurting rather than helping your investment selection. Further, your IQ tested too high (you are too smart). As a result you try to complicate and outsmart a perfect system (the investment markets), and over time have developed some tough habits to break.

You probably scoffed at much of what I just said. How can your brain actually hinder your investment selection? Read on and you'll see. Once you accept what I say you will realize that greatness is closer than you think. It's quite simple: Follow the theme throughout the book, use it as a frame, and you will see how you can harness greatness and pounce at will. Once you step out of your own way (and pounce where I direct), great wealth is all but yours to take.

## WEALTH AND INVESTING

... And so it begins.

So far this morning I have enjoyed a cup of coffee and had the pleasure of taking my beautiful daughters to school. When I returned home I admired my nice landscaping before sitting down to complete this chapter.

Based on how I describe a typical morning, would you believe that you are reading the words of a predator—an investment predator? You wouldn't realize that I run a firm that manages hundreds of millions of dollars. And when I get to the "main" office later today, there will be no shouting, craziness, or the like.

As I am writing this book, the news headlines are alarming. I recently read that the homes of José Canseco and a California congressional representative have recently entered into foreclosure, and that Ed McMahon was facing foreclosure. Unemployment is over 6.7 percent. The consumer is still hopeful and despair does not yet reign supreme. One of two things will happen. The markets will rally around good news, causing a brief hiccup in a downward trend, and start moving higher, saving the bigger downturn for another day. Or, what is more likely, the negativity will throw us right into bear market territory, causing serious corrections until despair rules the day.

Like my dog, Charlie, I lick my lips as if waiting to receive a treat. My heart beats faster. I wait. I am an investment predator. Under either scenario, I feel confident that the prey will be mine. My prize: positive investment results.

## LET ME TELL YOU A STORY, A NEAR TRAGEDY . . .

These great friends of mine got married about ten years ago. Peter is exceptionally bright, makes over $200,000 a year, and is extremely well read. His wife, Rose, is also exceptionally gifted, earns less than half of what Peter makes, but is also very well read, and is very much in love with Peter. The only thing is (isn't there always a thing?), Peter gets very excited and emotional when it comes to his money. It is not that he spends excessively, but, because of his intellect and drive, he believes he is a great investor.

Right after their marriage, with excess income, Peter saw just how well the technology stocks were doing. "Truly," as he would say, "we are living in a new world, a world of the tech revolution. Old investment rules are changing. To not be part of this would be foolish." Rose was not so sure, but Peter was convincing. "Rose, our friends look up to me and they are making the money off of this and we are not. It is time to strike." Rose acquiesced. Around the beginning of 1999 they opened a brokerage account and began to buy some of the Internet stocks they heard so much about. Within a few months they were up almost 25 percent! Peter was so happy, he changed his 401(k) around to invest almost exclusively in technology.

Just after the beginning of 2000, a few of the stocks dropped fairly hard. Rose was worried. Peter said that he had done his research and knew this was "part of the process," and that when things like this happened, it was time to "load up and get quality names on sale." What was left of their savings he plowed back into the same stocks that dropped.

By 2001 Peter and Rose had lost their life savings. Thank goodness, however, they still had their jobs, and their income would allow them to rebuild. They had learned an extremely valuable lesson. Never again would they invest foolishly, and probably not ever again in the stock market.

By 2003 some of Peter's friends were buying rental real estate. Interest rates were so low, sometimes you could buy for "no money down." *This* was the perfect investment, Peter told Rose. "What is the worst that could happen? We will sell it for what we paid. Real estate really doesn't drop, and if so we can rent it out. Even if it just breaks even at first, over the next several years the real estate will produce cash flow and fund our retirement! But the big money is in buying these preconstruction homes and condo conversions, and once they are complete, we sell them." Peter and Rose had saved some money between 2001 and 2003. Plus, there was still a little bit left in Peter's 401(k) that he could borrow against. Over the next three years they bought three properties, using all the money they had. And then, interest rates began to rise. Real estate began to soften. They decided to sell their properties and take the money and run. However, they priced the real estate high. Interest rates rose further. Real estate basically crashed. And then, a recession ensued.

They had no choice: Not being able to make payments, they walked away. Every property went into foreclosure.

This is a tragic story. But the worst part is that Peter and all the other Peters in this world will continue to make these mistakes over and over and over. What are the mistakes? Not investing in what you know? Partly. Not investing with a plan? Partly. Not having a sell strategy. That, too. Investing alongside the herd. Yes, that was yet another mistake.

Although this is a tragic story, thankfully all was not lost. Early on, Rose came to me (I told you we were friends), explaining Peter's enthusiasm and her concern for how they were going about investing. She wanted to invest and grow wealthy but truly felt they were just "running with the herd." And they really needed a strategy. She didn't want to tell Peter, because he would have convinced her to go "all in" with what they were doing.

It turned out Rose had some money as a result of an inheritance, and she contributed 100 percent of her raises to an investment plan. She embraced the teachings of how to truly pounce and take advantage of bubbles and manias. She built an investment system and religiously stuck to it, instead of buying, holding, and forgetting. She became an investment predator. She saw that technology was a man-made bubble. She also realized when it got too cheap. She relied on her knowledge that bear markets end, and waited patiently to pounce on this bear, riding the next bull. Real estate was the next bubble. She stepped aside, focusing her attention on other areas of her plan.

Quietly, Rose had exponentially grown their net worth despite Peter's follies. Because of the volatility and chaos on Wall Street, she was able to use the inefficiencies created by the herd to her advantage. Tragedy averted!

Don't you love happy endings?

## JUST ONE THING

Woven into all of the ideas, strategies, and investment disciplines in this book is one common theme. It is amazingly simple, yet it can be elusive. Please understand and embrace this concept, then build a strategy to exploit it.

The concept is: People move markets and economies. We move the markets to extremes, whether an overall stock, an asset class (for example, real estate), or the economy as a whole. We move from fair value to overvalued and then back to fair value to undervalued. People create markets. People acting rationally will always lead to the irrational, meaning, we fool ourselves into believing our actions are rational, when in truth the actions are the exact opposite. "Honey, let's buy an income property. The bank is offering five percent financing with no dollars down. If we can't get it rented, we can always sell for a higher price than we paid." This is an example of rational, irrational thinking. That's it. Embrace this and thrive in any situation.

## POUNCE SUMMARY

If this book were a thriller, you'd have to wait until the climactic last chapter to learn all its secrets. But it's not, so here's the last page. Read these rules now, and then read the rest of the book to learn how to apply them.

## POUNCE RULES OF SUCCESS

1. Train your brain. Remove the emotion and randomness from your decision making in order to realize investment success.

2. Understand the Power of 3 (P3). By utilizing the three investment indicators—Value, Economic Direction, and Investor Psyche/Market Behavior—you can begin to determine the direction of the market. From this, you can create a portfolio that should thrive *because* of crazy markets and erratic behavior.

3. Position yourself to Profit because of volatile markets. Understand the traits of the three different markets—bull markets, bear markets, and neutral markets, which I will refer to as the Void—and manipulate lulls or violent economic swings to pounce and profit.

4. Truly understand that markets are perfect and that people create bubbles, bear markets, and bull markets. This reality will allow you to weave among the masses, pounce in, pounce out, and never be affected by the irrationality of people. In fact, you will use the masses to your advantage, not your detriment.

5. You can never know for certain when a bear market will end or a bull market will begin. You will not know if the next hot sector is emerging markets or commodities or something else. You will, instead, trust your indicators and your system. They will tell you what to do and where to invest. By keeping tight control of your system, and by not allowing your intuition to dominate, unchecked, your investment decisions, you will flush out which investments you should have, and at what times, and disregard the rest.

Embrace and act upon the instructions and lessons herein—and you can more than succeed. You can thrive and realize greatness.

## THE ULTIMATE GOAL

Imagine sitting on a rock, high above a great jungle. The view is magnificent. It's amazing how clear everything appears. You can see the cheetah chasing the gazelle. As the gazelle zigzags back and forth you notice how futile the effort is. The cheetah is singular in focus, not attempting to match the zigs and zags in the process, but steadily gaining on his prey, ready to pounce.

Over in the lake you watch as the alligator silently floats upon the surface as the confident birds move ever closer. You see the kill even before it happens—there was never a doubt.

And as for you, watching this with the clarity this view provides, you could simply pounce at will—wherever or whenever you wish.

The ultimate goal of Pounce is for you to become one with wealth and investing. Take the emotions, fear, and uncertainty out of your investment model. Create your personal Alpha Investment Platform. Finally, develop enhanced skills that will allow you to minimize the unwanted noise as it is associated with investments, and with precision to pounce at will.

As the chaos enfolds around me, while foreclosures and unemployment climb, and a few people are making untold riches in commodities and overseas, I see it all, act on what I desire, and sleep well knowing that I am king of the jungle. Bubbles, manias, herds, and irrational exuberance are all potential opportunities to Pounce.

I know you want "the good stuff," so I will summarize salient points at the beginning of each chapter. I caution you, however, that without the insight and knowledge to support the summary, you may walk into the dangerous jungle without being fully skilled.

So, please read the entire book.

Investing will take the knowledge to create strategy, the courage to adhere to your strategy, and the ability to execute this system. Leave your emotions at the door and follow a system that is 80 percent objective and 20 percent subjective.

**BOOK ONE**

# READY

## Gather Your Resources

**IN THE MOVIE** *The Matrix*, Keanu Reaves has just learned that he has been living in a computer-generated "matrix." The world he thought he knew was simply a computer program. The "real people" who saved him in fact loaded him up with various computer programs to better compete in the matrix. They programmed him with fighting skills and weapons knowledge. I'm going to do exactly the same thing. I will load you up with all the knowledge you require to become the ultimate investment predator, nimbly moving between chaotic markets and economies, feeding and moving on.

Book One will help you better understand how to call the direction of the market and the market bias. We learn the P3 Power Indicators and how they will guide us in building the ultimate investment platform: the Personal Pounce Platform.

Book One teaches us about our brains and what triggers will help us become more successful investment predators, and what actually hinders us.

The theme is as clear as it is effective: Success is achieved through a system. Investing is not intuitive, as people tend to be. Investing is counterintuitive. Our brains should be busy executing the system, not trying to "decide" if we are making the right decisions to grow wealth.

This is the battle we focus on in Book One. In Books Two and Three we will learn the system: Pounce. Simply stated, most investment systems and investment managers are stagnant. They create a system, and hope it works in flat markets, during the market peak, and even during bull and bear markets. Pounce does no such thing. Pounce is disciplined. It is easy, but it is dynamic.

# 1

## Assess Your Kingdom

**PROFITABLE POUNCE IN EVERY SITUATION**

In a minute you will peek into Pounce. By way of summary, let me tell you what I like about Pounce. It is simple, yet advanced and smart, it works. If you do it right, you need to master only three ideas:

1. Hold one investment meeting (even if it's with yourself) once per month—and trade only once per month.
2. Summarize three market direction indicators.
3. Implement the investment strategies provided in Book Three into your Personal Pounce Platform.

That is it. I don't mean to oversimplify the system. You will have to gather information every month for your meeting, even if your meeting is just with yourself. It might take an hour or two. Subsequently, you will probably be making a few trades every month.

What you do not have to do is very much in the way of internal debate (with yourself). You do not need to make any gut decisions or
rely on instinct. The investment screens will tell you when to buy
and sell. If you can adhere to the discipline, you will love Pounce.

If a strategy exists regarding money and wealth, it is likely I have
studied it and might even have tried it. I have found the analytical
books to be too complicated for most people to follow—and probably too smart to work. All the "fluff" books are just that—they feel
soft and nice, make us feel good at the end of the day. The fluff
books deliver the same message—we get it! Right? Wrong! You are
still searching. The premises of these books are fine; live modestly,
invest your money for the long term, buy some rental property and
some solidly performing long-term mutual funds, diversify, and live
happily ever after.

This is wrong, wrong, wrong.

First, it is BORING! This just doesn't cut it for me. I want to
live a fabulous life. I don't want an average existence. I need
more. Think back to Rose. She was able to carry out her investment plan on limited time and resources. Life should not be
consumed by investing. In fact, being too involved will have a
deleterious effect, as it may cause you to make emotional decisions. As I've said, our system is based on making, if necessary,
changes to your portfolio once per month—and only once, and
only if necessary.

The second problem with these books is the fact that life inter-
rupts your plans; kids, recessions, energy crises, a longer life span,
high medical costs, possibly issues we have not even begun to think
about yet—food or water shortages maybe?

Third, this buy-and-hold approach is not going to be very

lucrative in the absence of a long-term bull market. From the beginning of 2000 until the middle of 2008, the Standard & Poor's 500 Index has been actually down. I think the same may be true over the next eight years. If you had eight years without growth in your money, that would be a serious setback. (The Standard & Poor's 500 Index is our benchmark. When I refer to the "market" going up or down, I am referring to this index.)

## Best Defense—Strong Offense

Seeing that the best defense is a strong offense, I opted out of the average investment system, and so should you. Instead of being a "defensive" investor, I decided to go on the offensive. I want to act, not react. Basically, I want to make profitable and wise investment choices throughout my life. I want to actually be positioned to take advantage of chaos, trying economies, bull and bear markets alike. To accomplish this I have become a predator . . . an investment predator, prepared and trained to pounce at will.

But there is a catch: Training for predatory wealth is not automatic. The training will require you to dig just a bit deeper to realize your true pouncing potential. If you can commit to a slightly more active role with your investments, and a bit of education, you are more than halfway toward greatness.

One of the areas of further education is going to be in your ability to execute an investment screen. Pounce will give you all the parameters. Pounce will show you how and where (on the Internet) to execute the screen. It really is quite simple; however, it's understandably intimidating if you have never built an investment screen before. Think back to the first jump in the lake on that hot, sticky day. The anxiety and fear of the unknown were quickly replaced with the elation and gratification of hitting the water. Don't psyche yourself out.

Once you are willing to admit your brain has been holding you back, we will get on with sharpening your investment skills. When you read chapter 3, "Animal Instincts," you will learn a little bit about our brains and how they are wired incorrectly to help us be successful investors. Make no mistake about it. The skill and talent are there, but your instinct kicks in—either to help you survive or to give you pleasure—and overrides what your true abilities are. Once we get beyond that . . .

The Plan

As mentioned earlier, here are the three Power Indicators (P3). These indicators are going to give you direction. They are:

- ✓ Value
- ✓ Economic Direction
- ✓ Investor Psyche/Market Behavior

Upon mastering these directional indicators, you will have the power of sight—the sight to watch the trend of the investment landscape. The direction of the P3 indicators will give you the ability to choose the bias of your Personal Pounce Platform; bullish, bearish, or neutral.

With this valuable knowledge, you will sharpen your claws and be prepared to pounce.

In Book Three you will be presented with different investment strategies—Rising Stars, Fallen Angels, Top Gun, Market Neutral hedging, and others. You will use these strategies in your Personal Pounce Platform. You will be provided the key, the screen to each strategy. I have designed Pounce so you can go to your computer, screen what I tell you to screen, and buy and sell based on the result. It is objective and simple. No longer do you bite your nails deciding how you should invest, or worry if the recession will get worse or the bull market will end. We'll incorporate this into your investment strategy. You just need to implement it.

Your Personal Pounce Platform is an investment platform designed to maximize your success using three strategies. The strategies vary, depending on the direction of the investment landscape. The Personal Pounce Platform has three systems, each of which has 33 percent of your investment capital to start. We'll go into all this in much more detail in Book Three, but here's an overview:

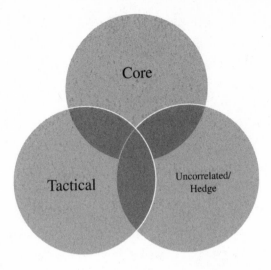

| CORE<br>System 1 | TACTICAL<br>System 2 | UNCORRELATED/HEDGE<br>System 3 |
| --- | --- | --- |
| • Rising Stars<br>• Pounce for Income<br>and Growth | • Top Gun | • Fallen Angels<br>• BuyWrite<br>• Market Neutral<br>• Modified Market<br>Neutral<br>• Pair Trade<br>• Ultra Short |

## THE PERSONAL POUNCE PLATFORM

The investment strategies reviewed in Book Three will be utilized within your investment model, the Personal Pounce Platform. Using the data you collect from the P3 Indicators, you will bias your Personal Pounce Platform to a bullish, bearish, or neutral stance.

Your Personal Pounce Platform is your frame. All decisions that you may face regarding investments will be filtered through it. This platform is divided into three sections—go figure! I love it. Simple, neat, and effective. The Personal Pounce Platform is designed to embrace, and thrive during, varying markets and economic scenarios.

The Personal Pounce Platform is not a trading system. Rather it is a long-term investment platform designed to help you act, not react. The strategy calls for you to review the platform once a month to determine what, if any, alterations need to be made.

The Personal Pounce Platform is divided into three parts (known as systems):

System 1—Core
System 2—Tactical
System 3—Uncorrelated/Hedge

*System 1: Core.* This is designed to search for companies that offer superior growth for each particular market. Although many systems attempt to accomplish the same goal and mimic similar systems, two distinct differences exist with regard to your Core. The first difference is how your criteria change based on your P3 indicators. For example, if all three indicators are bullish, you will allocate a higher percentage to your Core system. Or if P3 is trending bearish, dividends and stock buybacks would be more important. The second variation is the fact that this is not a "buy-and-hold forever" system. At any point that a company does not meet the system's rigorous screening process, the stock will be sold. Your Core system will seek primarily to invest in individual stocks.

Within Core, I have created two investment strategies. The first strategy is called Rising Star. The second is Pounce for Income and Growth. You will see that each strategy performs exceptionally well. Each strategy is objective, requiring you only to run a screen during your monthly Pounce meeting to determine which investments will be bought and sold. And each strategy will always be present within Core.

*System 2: Tactical.* This will expose you to an entirely different asset class. The system will primarily utilize Exchange Traded Funds (ETFs). It takes the approach that regardless of the economy or the type of market (bull, bear, or neutral), leadership will rise to the top. Leadership may be expressed through industry or sector performance.

This system will utilize our Top Gun investment strategy for tactical investing. In this regard you will screen for the "best" sector within the Standard & Poor's 500 Index. You will screen for the "best" global sector. You will screen for the "best" sector based on size (large, cap, mid-cap, or small cap). Once you find the best, with a few simple rules you will buy this sector and hold it until it is no longer "the best." You will understand what the Pounce definition of "the best" is in Book Three.

*System 3: Uncorrelated/Hedge.* This is the portion of your portfolio that has the ability to zig when the market zags. Based on the P3 reading, you have the ability to bet that certain markets, sectors, and industries will experience negative returns, giving you the opportunity to pounce on the bubble. You can invest in various securities that will bet that a certain sector or market will drop in value as well as invest in specific investment strategies that should do well if the market stays flat for extended periods. We'll review these strategies, including Fallen Angels and Pair Trades, later.

Many superior strategies exist to take advantage of markets that move up and down over extended periods. Yet few individual investors understand these strategies or utilize them. Without utilizing these strategies you have all the weight on one end of your seesaw. This is not prudent, at best. Today that stops. Today, you get access to everything.

## FACT VS. FICTION

Do you think Warren Buffett invests like Peter and Rose? Probably not. Warren Buffett has consistently, and for many years, enjoyed a return on his company stock, Berkshire Hathaway, in excess of the S&P 500, something very few investors do.

This is accomplished through his predatory skills and his pouncing ability. When the companies that insured municipal bonds flirted with bankruptcy (due to investing in a bunch of subprime loans that went belly-up), Buffett offered to bail them out. Was this an act of charity? Absolutely not! The deal tentatively proposed that Buffett would give the insurance companies the financing to stay afloat (which was really all they needed since the municipal bonds they were insuring were not defaulting), and in turn he would own a large percentage of the insurance company and most of their revenue—regardless of whether or not they made a profit. Virtually a no-lose deal. That is a perfect example of a predatory pounce. Similar actions were initiated after devastating hurricanes and other natural disasters.

The fact is, great investors take a proactive approach and realize that greatness is realized through turbulence, because of people's psyche and their overreactions. Great investors relish mispriced securities. They realize that often it takes adversity and it may be uncomfortable as well as unpopular, but having a system they rely on to invest during turbulent times is what makes them great.

## WHAT DO YOU EXPECT?

What I expect is to create a system that will direct me to more winning investments than losing investments. I expect this system to do well in both up and down markets.

Over the next twenty years, we will experience longer lifetimes, inflation, recessions, and bull and bear markets. Many market watchers think we will be lucky to make 6 percent per year on our investments. I think this is half right. I think that the markets, based on long-term trends, historic valuation averages, and available capital, will be lucky to make 6 percent.

We will have much fodder for doom-and-gloom scenarios—food and water shortages, labor issues, and supply constraints for other commodities, to name a few.

The future, of course, is unknown. Yet the unknown is what excites me; it does not worry me. I have no idea, nor do I wish to predict, what the S&P will return over the next twenty years. It really does not concern me. My system also is not a system that states, "We will seek to earn a consistent return of x percent per year." That is silly. What is not silly is to state that I will use market chaos, bubbles, and people's shortsighted emotional decisions for opportunity.

To me a great investment system is one that is right at least 60 percent of the time (preferably 70 percent) and insures that my positive trades go higher more frequently than my negative trades go lower. Whatever the future throws at us, there is an opportunity to pounce. If Warren Buffett can find ways to make money off a real estate debacle, subprime investments, and hurricanes, you should be able to as well.

## HOW CAN YOU PROFIT WHEN THE MARKETS ARE DOWN?

What is a bear market? Forget the textbook definition. A bear market is a market that investors sell to an extreme, oversold territory. If you rode the roller coaster all the way down, the negative return would likely wipe out much of your profits (assuming you had profits from the preceding up market cycle). However, a bear market creates two powerful opportunities. First, it creates lists of companies ready for a pounce. It makes your rational job that much easier. Second, it creates opportunities to find companies that excel during and *because* of the bear market. I have always believed in the Top 20 Percent.

Consider the S&P. These are 500 stocks grouped together to create an index. I steadfastly believe that I need only the top 20 percent in order to be successful. I don't need 400 stocks that are what I consider to be inferior investment choices. Just give me the best 20 percent, and whether we are experiencing a bull or a bear market, I should do well. If you think about it logically, there have to be at least 100 companies that are doing well *because* of adverse market conditions, right? This is contrary to popular belief that when markets are down *everything* is down.

Recently, during an analyst meeting, my colleague Eric Hoffman shattered that belief. Eric ran numerous studies and found that I was slightly off. Take 2001 as an example. The S&P lost 12.6 percent, but guess what? Two hundred nineteen stocks were up that year!

The next year was worse. In 2002 the S&P was down 21.9

percent. But 138 stocks were up! That means just over 27 percent of the stocks were higher in 2002. You can do this during most bear markets and find similar results.

The next logical question is, were there any repeated patterns for stocks that outperformed? Did certain sectors outperform others consistently or did the winning stocks have a lower price-to-earnings ratio, or some other indicator?

The answer is yes, there were trends, but this is a dangerous way to consider the data. If I told you that, on average, consumer staples outperformed other sectors, you might run out and buy stocks of companies selling consumer staples. This is statistics at its purest. But during the next bear market, staples may not be the best performer. Please do not manage money based on this type of analysis.

The similarities or common themes that will give a pounce investor an advantage to a winning investment strategy are embedded in the strategies themselves, which you will learn. You will learn what I feel is important and what the common patterns and similarities are, such as companies that exceed earnings guidance.

## DOES POUNCE WORK?

Yes. I believe it does. I believe it works big. In fact, I created a hypothetical variation of the Personal Pounce Platform, and to the extent possible, back-tested this platform beginning January 1, 2000. A few variations have been made, and you have to remember that back-testing can sometimes produce erroneous results. That being said, consider the chart comparing Pounce to the Standard & Poor's 500 Index.

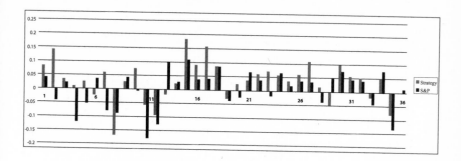

The above graph illustrates the variation in up and down periods (quarters) for Pounce and the S&P. The S&P is black; Pounce is gray. Pounce was up more and more often than the S&P. When Pounce was down, it was not down as much as the S&P.*

Not only did Pounce outperform S&P, but you can see that it outperformed in most quarters, providing an important consistent return.

The total return measures roughly 292 percent cumulative, or just over 14 percent annually. The Standard & Poor's 500 Index was flat for the same period.

## HOW SHOULD ADDITIONAL INVESTMENT STRATEGIES FIT WITH POUNCE?

You no doubt encounter daily many seemingly exciting investment strategies. Some are fads and will be outdated before long.

---

* This is a hypothetical portfolio and hypothetical return. Back-testing a strategy could produce difference results that are different from audited performance numbers. This investment platform invested in five separate investment strategies and did not rebalance for each strategy. The strategies that were used were Core, Rising Stars, and Pounce for Income and Growth. For tactical, the only strategy that was used was the S&P sector with the highest earning revision for uncorrelated/hedge system, the Modifed Market Neutural was the only investment strategy used.

Others are great long-term strategies. You hear of Elliott Wave and the Dow Theorists, pure technicians who focus solely on the charts and technical stock patterns. You will find people who prefer to buy stocks with low price-to-earnings and price-to-sales ratios and people who will only buy stocks reaching new highs. Strategies exist that tell you to "Sell in May and Go Away" or not to own certain stocks during a presidential election year.

My problem with many of these concepts is that they *may* work, some of the time, in certain situations. I think they may offer a good strategy but not a complete wealth system. These strategies usually tackle one specific aspect of the market. Unfortunately for them (but fortunately for the Pounce system), every market and market cycle is different. In the short term, everything is random and barely predictable. In the long term, everything is predictable and nothing has changed—it really isn't different this time. Let me save you some time. Create a system and follow it consistently. Do not chase fads du jour and you will be much happier.

Pounce mainly uses familiar investments such as stocks and mutual funds, and some slightly more exotic vehicles such as Exchange Traded Funds. But we will focus on investing in just enough stocks, not too many or too few. Too many stocks could turn your portfolio into a closet index fund, and could cost you a higher percentage in trading fees. Too few stocks will not create the proper diversification you need, and could also cost you too high a percentage in trading fees.

Your Personal Pounce Platform will divide your investments into three systems; Core, Tactical, and Uncorrelated/Hedge. System 1, Core, is well suited for an individual stock portfolio. System 2, Tactical, is well suited for ETFs or mutual funds and can be utilized with relatively small amounts of assets. System 3, Uncorrelated/Hedge, would need higher amounts of capital if you try to create your own hedge system, but a relatively small amount of assets if you utilize ETFs. I think using ETFs could be very cost-effective and sensible here. We'll get into all these details later.

## SUMMARY

Your kingdom is before you. Prior to jumping in for the Pounce, you must hone your skills. Stay with Book One and immerse yourself in the law of this jungle. Master your mind. Study the P3 Power Indicators, and be prepared to sharpen your claws on the investment strategies to come.

# 2

## Run with the Bulls, Pounce on the Herd

### BOOMS AND BUSTS AND EVERTHING IN BETWEEN

It has been said that you can't predict when a recession will come, or when a CEO will rip a company off, or if a terrible hurricane will cause a building to collapse. Our lives are comprised of a series of random events.

This is all true. You can't with amazing accuracy predict anything of the sort. THANK GOD! For the true predator, it is the unpredictable that creates the short-term inequities we seek to capitalize on. This is what creates inefficiencies. As I've said, markets are perfect, people are not. I never, ever want anything bad to happen to anybody. But my job is to uncover inequities and cracks and to pounce upon the prey when it is presented.

So if the country is wrapped up in the oil crisis, let us figure out how to profit from it. Is the latest version of mad cow disease affecting the beef industry, or avian flu affecting the poultry industry, or floods in Iowa threatening to affect the corn crop dramatically? Maybe the hype about mad cow disease creates an opportunity to buy stocks of steak restaurants. Or perhaps the perception of avian flu will create a buying opportunity for poultry producers. I'm willing to bet there is a pounce in each of these situations—every single one.

There is much you will learn about money and investing, but of everything you need to remember, it all boils down to two salient facts, the only two constants I've found when it comes to investing. And with these two facts, I think it's possible to create profitable investment strategies.

The first fact is: People create markets. Whatever people are willing to pay for a security is what it is worth. The definitions that we will review during the bull/bear segment of Pounce are fine for reference purposes, but let me tell you the true definitions of a bull and a bear market. A bull market is when *people* overshoot to the upside and a bear market is when *people* exaggerate the downside. Knowing that people create markets, and always overdo it (to the upside or the downside) should provide an opportunity to take advantage and exploit this fact.

The second fact is: Everything is based on value. If something is undervalued, it will most likely move to overvalued. Once overvalued, it will most likely move back to undervalued. Cheap is not value. Stocks that go down in value often go down for a reason, and even if the sell-off is overdone, buying a stock just because it is cheap is as risky as, if not more risky than, buying a stock that is too expensive. Value is not cheap.

## RUNNING WITH THE BULLS

My pretend sister Nikki came to me and told me her friend was going to Spain to run with the bulls. She feared for his life and asked if I would talk to him. Since there was no chance I wanted this lamb as a brother-in-law I was hesitant, thinking: What a way to get rid of him! Relax, I am a predator, but I am just kidding! Anyway, I agreed.

I asked the young lad why he was running with the bulls. He said it would be a thrill and his friends seemed excited—it's something to tell his children and grandchildren. "What do you mean?" I asked. He went on to try to convince me how he thought this would be a great experience for him and his friends.

"What about the risk" I asked? He shrugged it off, as if the risk was for somebody else. I pressed further, "Seriously, you could die." He said he didn't think so. So, I asked a few more questions: Did you study the number of deaths? How many people are seriously injured? He admitted that he didn't know these answers. It dawned on me. For the first time I truly was beginning to understand the relationship between people and their wealth and investments. Like an attorney questioning the defendant on the witnesses stand, knowing he backed the defendant into a corner, I picked up steam and crafted my next question. "Forgetting all else, would you still do it if you knew you *would* be maimed and die?"

"No! Of course not," he replied.

I felt like saying, "I rest my case."

The first mistake people make in investing is not taking the time to understand risk. We need to understand why we are doing something and the upside or the downside to the decision.

Think about your investments. Would you make the same decisions if you *knew* you would lose money? Probably not. Yet you still made the investment. I do not believe you know risk. In one context, risk is never knowing all of the potential outcomes that a certain action (or transaction) could result in. This is potentially why all my expensive math guys can't make my portfolios more money. You can't predict everything. So, back to risk. Since everything cannot be predicted and you cannot create a statistical probability for everything, go on this premise: You are predisposed to losing money.

But I say: Be aggressive and do not lose money.

Now what the heck does that mean? That means, create a system that allows you to thrive when "reality strikes." Life will happen. The unexpected will happen. I invest based on finding the trouble. I'll go in, expecting trouble to come after me. That way, whatever surprises are in store, I have developed a system to either mitigate the trouble or thrive because of it (not in spite of it). If you are without a system such as your Personal Pounce Platform, I would suggest you have not truly faced risk yet.

The second issue that Nikki's friend has is not knowing why he chooses to do this run. For himself? For his friends? For his grandchildren? This is an example of the second biggest mistake in investing: not knowing how to use the herd mentality rather than be abused by it. You can make this mistake if you don't know what you are expecting from your investments. If you are not confident when you should buy, when to sell, and what the expectation is, then you should not be investing.

Have you ever seen Disney's *The Jungle Book*? My daughters and I loved it. There is one song I still can't get out of my head. King Louie, the orangutan, is talking about Mowgli, the "Man Cub," and says, "I wanna be like you, I wanna talk like you, walk like you . . ." Research has proven that babies begin mimicking facial expressions soon after birth. So why are we so surprised when everyone mimics everyone else's investment decisions?

I have read dozens of articles that refer to the herd. Most of these articles suggest that you not invest with the rest of the herd. Well, this is just wrong. If you don't invest with the herd, how can you make money? You need more buyers than sellers, and buyers buying bigger amounts, to drive a price higher. What I think they mean is be careful if the herd gets out of control, because when the herd takes off and leaves, you will be the one coming crashing back down to reality—only with a lot less money.

Bubbles will burst. You will wonder, like Peter, "Why did I buy those tech stocks, that real estate?" During the Internet mania of 1995–2001, a Purdue University study said that companies could get a 53 percent bump in their stock price simply by switching to a dot-com name. From XYZ to XYZ.com. Investors were so blinded by, and running so fast with, the herd, individual thought was all but nonexistent.

I read a research study by two Stanford researchers and one at Duke.* They write, "Investors fear most being poor when everyone around them is rich." They found that even if people know a stock is overpriced, their fear of doing something different from their peers and potentially losing out makes them move in ever-greater numbers to the swelling investment bubble. Herding also provides a buffer when the bubble bursts. "If everyone loses his or her money together, it's perceived as not as bad as if you lose alone."

Let me tell you my take on running with the herd. Most people will tell you never to invest with the herd. I don't agree with this. Instead of running as fast as I can so the bull doesn't maim me, I think I'll find a way to jump on the back of the bull, ride it for a

---

* Peter M. DeMarzo, Ron Kaniel, and Ilan Kremer, "Relative Wealth Concerns and Technology Bubbles."

bit, and jump off when I'm ready. It's much easier than running away all the time (and much faster, I would think). You have heard the saying that you don't want to go a restaurant where there are no cars in the lot? Well, I like going to great restaurants. I just don't like to wait. Instead I'll go get the early bird special. I want to eat a good meal (at a good price), and leave as the herd rushes in. This analogy works just fine in investing, too. We'll come back to this when we talk about investing in Rising Stars.

## PREDATORS AND RISK

Let's chat a bit more about risk. It would be fair to assume that being an investment predator means I am willing to take risk. Although you may assume that—and of course, there is an element of risk in anything we do—I abhor risk. I do not like being wrong, being taken advantage of, or losing money.

The other day I met with a really nice guy. He said he wanted to allocate his portfolio for aggressive growth. So I gave him a questionnaire to fill out to ascertain his risk tolerance. One question was, How much would you be willing to lose? He looked at the question and said, "I know there is risk, but I don't want to lose money." Got it! Most investors are *willing to accept risk, unless the risk is realized.* Just like Nikki's friend.

Risk is the fact that you cannot quantify or assume every probability. But what you can do is account for as much as you can to minimize what can't be quantified.

Do you think it's riskier to buy stocks hitting new fifty-two-week highs or fifty-two-week lows? Most of us would say the stocks hitting new highs are the riskier choice. If you measure volatility risk or deviation (betas and deviation), this may be true. But, in fact, stocks that hit new highs tend to outperform those stocks hitting new lows over the following twelve months.*

I think the risk is not investing with the leadership on the way up and then not knowing when to get off the ride. Most investors focus so strongly on buying at the right time that they forget that selling at the right time is equally important.

Further, risk and return do not go hand in hand, as is popularly theorized. Not all bear markets occur simultaneously, not all economies experience recessions at the same time. I believe that, by using a three-pronged investment platform—the Personal Pounce Platform—you can take advantage of varying markets to consistently build wealth without excessive risk. Can you lose money? Yes. Are there events that are not thought of yet? Of course. However, a true system should be able to take advantage of these events and anomalies as they occur.

Should you be concerned about the various risk measurements you might read about, such as standard deviation, beta, R-Squared? The answer is, yes to an extent, but do not be overly concerned. Usually, one compares the rise or fall in value of an investment to a benchmark (the S&P being a common benchmark). Deviation is the up and down movement away from the benchmark. A high deviation means that the investment swings much higher or lower than the benchmark.

High deviation tends to represent the risk of owning a specific security. The overall concept is that the higher the risk (deviation), the higher the potential return, since the value could go up or down. In fact, I believe you should always measure the value of

---

* See Ken Stern, *Secrets of the Investment All-Stars* (New York: Amacom, 1999).

your total portfolio to that of a benchmark. If you are not beating the benchmark, you are doing something wrong. If your return is the same as the S&P 500 Index, but your risk as measured by deviation is higher, you are not performing as well as the S&P. In fact, it pays to be defensive when the indicators I'll discuss later are trending lower. Of course, risk could also be measured by market risk, stock market risk, and company risk. All of these are factors for you to consider in understanding your investments and how to mitigate risk. Again, do I give a great deal of consideration to this? Some. But truthfully, I focus on my Pounce Platform. I focus on beating the market, I focus on positive returns year after year. I focus on results.

Your most recent investing memory may be of a great, giant bull market that began in 1982 and ended in 2000. Many learned professionals assume we are years away from the beginning of another great bull. The markets dropped in 2000 and kept dropping for a few years. They enjoyed a great rally, and then reentered another cyclical bear market (a decline of at least 20 percent). Most investors that bought and held in 2000 are no better off than they were eight years ago. This is unacceptable. Yet this pattern could likely continue for many more years (see chapter 8, "Bulls, Bears, and More Foolishness"). This up and down pattern, although we may not be accustomed to it after such a long bull market, is actually not the aberration but rather the norm.

Do I know if the great bull will reemerge? No! And neither do you. Nor do I care to question what I cannot answer. Don't fear the cycles—embrace them. If not, I am afraid you will buy the index and emerge flat. Or, after counting tax and inflation, you may actually emerge from an extended investment period with a loss.

I went back and studied market returns using different starting points. Going back as far as 1959 until the end of 2007, I found that, except for brief periods in the late 1990s, average annualized, inflation adjusted, return over a twenty-year period often did not exceed 6 percent. Given that I think inflation will steadily increase (see futurist pounce projections), added to the fact that stocks are not extremely undervalued based on their long-term historic value measures, the next ten or so years are not likely to be incredibly profitable for a buy-and-hold investor.

If the next ten years are not profitable for a buy-and-hold investor, yet people live longer and at higher cost, I believe that, as investors, we are almost forced to develop predator pouncing skills. Buy and hold won't cut it.

Second, study after study has shown that investors do not make the gains that the index makes, or achieve published mutual fund returns, for that matter. Why is this? Because your intuition has you in survival and pleasure mode, prompting you to make decisions based on intuition. Unfortunately, as you will learn, the investment jungle is most often counterintuitive. I have found the best time to invest is when there is no hope and all around me are in despair. Somewhere in the back of your mind, your analytical mode knows this, but your survival mode kicks in. Relying on intuition, it gets you out of Dodge—at exactly the wrong time. Part of being a successful investment predator is learning the investment predator's animal instincts—the ability to quiet intuition down a bit and allow this intuition to work in partnership with your analytical side. One way of doing this is to have an investment system—the Personal Pounce Platform.

The same is true when asset values get too expensive. Other than intuition, your brain is designed to provide pleasure. It is extremely pleasurable to watch your investments go higher as the

## Annualized Returns of the S&P 500 Index—Nominal
### (looking backward)

| Period Ending: | ——— Number of Years ——— | | | | |
| --- | --- | --- | --- | --- | --- |
| | 10 | 15 | 20 | 25 | 30 |
| December 31, 1959 | 13.65% | | | | |
| December 31, 1964 | 8.95% | 11.45% | | | |
| December 31, 1969 | 4.39% | 6.46% | 8.92% | | |
| December 31, 1974 | −2.10% | 0.91% | 3.28% | 5.82% | |
| December 31, 1979 | 1.60% | 1.63% | 2.99% | 4.49% | 6.43% |
| December 31, 1984 | 9.33% | 4.06% | 3.46% | 4.19% | 5.25% |
| December 31, 1989 | 12.59% | 11.55% | 6.96% | 5.88% | 6.10% |
| December 31, 1994 | 10.63% | 10.14% | 9.98% | 6.64% | 5.79% |
| December 31, 1999 | 15.31% | 15.59% | 13.95% | 13.04% | 9.67% |
| December 31, 2004 | 10.19% | 8.56% | 10.41% | 10.16% | 10.05% |

## Annualized Returns of the S&P 500 Index—
### Inflation-Adjusted (looking backward)

| Period Ending: | ——— Number of Years ——— | | | | |
| --- | --- | --- | --- | --- | --- |
| | 10 | 15 | 20 | 25 | 30 |
| December 31, 1959 | 11.18% | | | | |
| December 31, 1964 | 7.26% | 9.40% | | | |
| December 31, 1969 | 1.83% | 4.04% | 6.40% | | |
| December 31, 1974 | −6.96% | −2.85% | −0.10% | 2.54% | |
| December 31, 1979 | −5.36% | −4.29% | −1.83% | 0.17% | 2.33% |
| December 31, 1984 | 1.86% | −2.83% | −2.65% | −0.99% | 0.55% |
| December 31, 1989 | 7.13% | 5.14% | 0.69% | 0.13% | 1.07% |
| December 31, 1994 | 6.81% | 5.33% | 4.30% | 0.92% | 0.41% |
| December 31, 1999 | 12.03% | 12.03% | 9.55% | 7.85% | 4.34% |
| December 31, 2004 | 7.58% | 5.62% | 7.19% | 6.22% | 5.38% |

herd takes the market to new, unsustainable heights. I think we are all smart enough to see this happen, and know we should take our gains, but our pleasure senses are very strong and hard to override. A system that does not focus on a buy-and-hold philosophy—one that is specific with minimal discretion—will allow you to act upon what you inherently know: Get off the ride before the fall back to reality occurs.

## PREDATORY INFORMATION: WHERE WE FIND THE INFORMATION TO DO OUR RESEARCH; AND, HOW TO CREATE A STOCK SCREEN

The strategies included in Pounce were designed to be used by anyone with a personal computer and/or access to a library. Virtually all the information that you need should be available on your PC.

You will notice that some of the strategies call for stock screening. Stock screening is a process that allows us to discover stocks that meet our criteria. Computers and the Internet have made this process much, much easier. Without having to understand necessarily why, I have found that screening stocks for certain important characteristics can help you objectively weed out companies that you should not even consider as possible investment candidates. Further, and used properly, using a stock screen in reverse will create an opportunity for an investor to determine when to "pounce off." Which could mean buying an investment that goes higher if underlying investments within that security drop.

The pounce investor must remember how very important stock screening is. First, it takes emotion out. It allows you to quickly and objectively determine which stocks make the cut, and which deserve to be cut. Screening tools are available free on popular Web sites such as MSN and Yahoo!. Many screens are free. You can screen based on basic parameters, or you can buy very expensive screening programs that cost a few years' worth of salary. Pounce investors use screens to sniff out important data relating to both fundamentals (a company's financial data) and technical information (the chart and technical patterns of stock-market behavior). So if you are in front of a computer, go right to moneycentral.msn.com. In the upper left column, click "Investing." Then click "Stock Screener" under "Stocks."

What you are looking at is a very simple stock screening tool. Although you can create a few basic screens with this, we need a bit more firepower. To get the firepower, you will see, on the lower right, "Supercharge Your Search." If you don't find it here, click on "Stock Power Searches" and "Deluxe Stock Screener" will be in a box on top. If you still don't see it search for "MSN Tool Box." This button will allow you to download. Once the screen is up under "Field Name" you can click on these fields to uncover all the screening possibilities. With this you can build a screen similar to what I have illustrated. This is an advanced stock screening tool—and it's free. Music to my ears as well. Click on this and download this software. You should now be viewing a screen that says "Deluxe Stock Screener." This simple tool will allow you to input the exact parameters Pounce has identified to be important tools for smart investing. It is an awesome tool that can take your investing to a whole new level. We'll use this throughout the book.

Take a few minutes and practice creating a screen or two. Perhaps skip forward to chapter 10, "Core: Rising Stars and Pounce for Income and Growth," and see if you can create the screens I discuss there. Virtually all this data is readily available to you.

In future chapters I'll discuss analyst earnings estimates and what to think if the company actually hits these estimates, exceeds them, or fails to achieve the estimated results. I'll discuss average sales and earnings for a period of years, whether a company pays a dividend, and other measures. You do not need to be an accountant to master this. In fact, although it would be great to understand how a company calculates its earnings, it is not necessary. What you need is consistency in what you track. This is more important, in many cases, than specifically what you track.

Screening is, to me, far more valuable in calling the direction of a stock than "tearing apart" a company's numbers. In fact, too much crunching of the numbers causes you to outguess your system, which is bad.

Although many of these Web sites do not offer the screening tools that we have been focusing on, each supplies information that the Pounce investor may need:

www.reuters.com/investing
www. moneycentral.msn.com
www.marketscreen.com
www.valueengine.com
www.economy.com
www.marketwatch.com
www.morningstar.com
www.finance.yahoo.com
www.valueline.com
www.standardandpoors.com
www.minyanville.com
www.amex.com
www.investors.com
www.ishares.ca/splash.do
www.nasdaq.com/structuredeq/nasdaq_etf_family.stm
www.powershares.com/home.aspx

www.spdrindex.com/
www.ssgafunds.com/
http://flagship.vanguard.com/VGApp/hnw/FundsVIPER
www.rydexfunds.com/index.shtml

## SUMMARY

Wealth is yours for the taking. Create a strategy, follow the discipline of the strategy, and integrate wealth planning. If it sounds easy, it truly is—with the luxury of the clarity Pounce delivers to you. Embrace the changes. Be ready for changing economies; violent, unexpected shifts. Always be ready to pounce. Will it take courage? Yes. Will it require that you take an active role? Yes. Those who say you can get rich by investing for the long term and forgetting about it are only telling half the story. You, on the other hand, want and deserve more. You want greatness.

# 3

## Animal Instincts

*"You must unlearn what you have learned."*
—YODA

## CHAPTER NOTES

1. You CAN beat the market.
2. By overthinking investment strategies, relying too heavily on intuition and emotions to interfere, people are decreasing their odds when playing the market. If you just said, "Not me," you proved my point.
3. Manage your investments and finances with minimal subjectivity and minimal enthusiasm—it is a methodical strategy. Develop a checklist that will help keep you on track. What you are attempting to do is nullify your intuition and coax your analytical brain forward.
4. Men's and women's inherent differences extend into the investing world. Combining their investing tendencies would be the basis for a perfect investment strategy.
5. Neuroeconomics focuses on understanding the reasons behind emotional choices made in investing.

## ANIMAL INSTINCTS—YOUR MIND IS PLAYING TRICKS ON YOU

Regardless of what you have learned, the first truth is it is possible to beat the markets.

Assume you have $10,000. Also assume I can see into the future and I explain that you have two choices. Choice A would provide a consistent 6 percent return for fifteen years. Choice B would provide a 15 percent upside return in year one, a 15 percent upside return in year two, and a 15 percent downside return in year three. This cycle would repeat for fifteen years. Which would you rather have?

Almost everyone picks Choice B, with those sexy 15 percent returns. But in fact Choice B earns an overall return of 5.6 percent, well under the consistent 6 percent return—and arguably not worth the risk.

---

### Scenario 1

Invest $10,000 for ten years. The first four years your money earns 10 percent per year. In the fifth year it loses 10 percent. Years six through nine, your money earns 10 percent and on the tenth year it loses 10 percent.

OR

### Scenario 2

Invest $10,000 and earn 6 percent.

### Answer:

Scenario 1 at the end of 10 years = $17,363
Scenario 2 at the end of 10 years = $17,900

---

It may surprise you that the consistency of the 6 percent return outperforms the sporadic return. I like this little test for a variety of reasons. First, I like it because it sobers a person up rather quickly. Maybe these big returns and killings you think you will make as an investor are not necessary. Nor do they happen often, as you become the prey instead of the predator. When markets go down, they go down usually to excess. When markets rise, they rise to excess. People create the inefficiencies. So imagine the ability to enjoy much of the upside of the market, with minimal downside. This truly is the goal of Pounce: to position your investments to take advantage of investment cycles, consistently adding a few chips to your side of the table.

The purpose of this chapter is to introduce you to a very important, newly understood (and ever-evolving) theory as to why your success has been limited regarding wealth accumulation and investing. It quite simply is your brain. Specifically, how it is wired. If you are thinking at this very moment, "I don't need this, let's get to meat," then this is for you. Please read and absorb.

In the case of investing, raw instincts—the very instincts that tell you when you are hungry or in danger—can limit your investment success. Neuroeconomics is proving this theory. The basic premise is that while you may make excellent emotional and instinctual decisions that help keep you alive, or give you pleasure, these decisions could actually be detrimental to you and your investment world.

Remember my friend Peter? Peter was intellectual and believed he was making rational decisions—almost (I say, "almost," because it's not quite the same) like a person who is intoxicated but believes he can drive home.

What do you think would happen if you removed emotion

from your investment equation? If you devised a system for investing and executed it, without your own gut instinct overriding it? What if you refused to react at the first signs of a potential profit or trouble? If you never loved or hated any of your investments? How would your investments do? My argument is that they would do great and you would be the ultimate predator.

You may be thinking: But I do research, I am calculated and rational, yet I still am not where I want to be. It's not how much more analysis you will do—most is research that will not help you create a return superior to the markets anyway. You don't need another chart, another scheme, another tip. You already have more than enough data to pounce.

The reason you have not reached the next level yet is you. It's not the market, or the fact that you failed to find the next great software that will ensure your success with investing, or that you had some big expenses of late. It's you. You will always have new expenses to contend with. The markets are perfect. People mess them up. Too much analysis and charting is going to cause lack of success (yes, you can over-research)—especially if you are looking in the wrong area. And time spent on all that research is going to take away from living—isn't that why we are doing all this, to enjoy life?

As Billy Joel sings, "Should I try to be a straight-A student? If you are then you think too much." I couldn't have put it better myself. What the Piano Man was trying to say is that you can be just as smart as the straight 'A' student and receive a lower grade. But you will not sacrifice any more of your sanity or valuable time. Or, in other words earning "straight As" does not necessarily make you smart. As, researching for many more hours, will not necessarily make you a more successful investor.

What I am saying is that you get in the way because your brain is constantly trying to survive and find pleasure. These activities often override your seemingly rational investment decisions. Again, think of Peter. Everything he did was well thought out and believed to be rational. Yet he still failed miserably.

Neuroeconomics is a fairly new field combining psychology, economics, and neuroscience. I find that it is shedding light on investing and behavior. I know this may sound a little New-Agey, but understanding why people act in certain capacities, run in herds, form bubbles, or take risky bets will make you a better investor—period!

Neureconomics studies how we make choices. It seeks to learn how our brain evaluates a decision, and how we truly interpret risk and rewards. Let's explore it a bit.

Please consider this next exhibit.

This is an important chart. In the summer of 2008, at the time this was printed, it argues a large rally might soon come in the stock

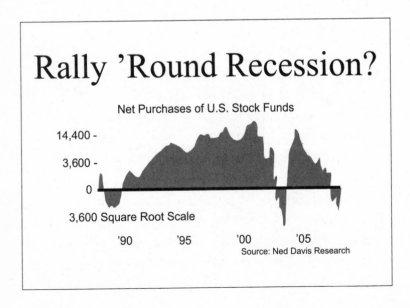

market. The graph shows when money is going into and out of mutual funds. If money is actually leaving mutual funds, the graph would drop to below zero. In the case of this graph, which begins in the middle 1980s, net outflows only occurred three times. The first was in the late 1980s. The stock market rallied for most of the 1990s. The second time mutual fund outflows turned negative was after the tech wreck in 2002. Thereafter the markets experienced a strong bull market. The third was during the middle of 2008. Net outflows in equity mutual funds have only occurred three times in the last twenty years. The last time it happened in 2002, the Dow Jones Industrial Average subsequently almost doubled. Adding fuel to the belief the market was about to rally, I would point out that investor cash is at an all-time high—just sitting on the sidelines waiting to be invested. Further, the broad-based Standard & Poor's 500 Index is trading at a *very* fair fourteen times earnings based on a rolling twelve months for estimates ending one year out. Oh, and by the way, profitability for corporations is quite high.

Okay, get the picture?

*Please Answer*

Based on the above paragraph, are you inclined to:

- **a.** Commit capital to equity investments?
- **b.** Sell your current equity investments?
- **c.** Do nothing?

Regardless of your answer, did you feel the answer was rational?

This is important. So many of us make an emotional decision that is seemingly so very rational. Using the above paragraph and your answer—regardless of the actual answer—you made what I call a seemingly rational answer that was really an irrational answer. You believe your answer to be clear, well thought through, and based on solid information and research. What actually happened was that you really didn't make that decision; your *reflexive* brain (we will explore the two parts of your brain) stepped in, like an override button, and made an intuitive, arguably brash, decision.

The brain actually works against your ability to logically create a superior investment model for one main reason—our natural predator instinct makes illogical, emotional decisions. Emotions are often not logical. Imagine the power if you could train your brain to make logically based emotional decisions!

I can just visualize the erudite engineer reading these pages and saying, "I am very rational, calculated, and make well-informed decisions." This is the point! Your decisions may be somewhat rational but are predominately emotional. This causes you to convince yourself the conclusion you create is logical, when it is not. Hang in there with me for a bit longer. I'll prove the point.

If you owned a stock that dropped 20 percent, would you:

**a.** Sell it
**b.** Hold it until it got back to where you bought it
**c.** Buy more

There is really not any one right answer—rather, what your investment discipline and investment platform dictates is the right answer. The real question is, why? It is imperative that you understand the reason you chose what you did. What drives your decision?

This experiment, taken from *Your Money & Your Brain*, by Jason Zweig, demonstrates how people sometimes base decisions on how they feel over what is logical:

> In this experiment, researchers instructed people to try picking a colored jellybean from either of two bowls. In the one on the left, 10% of the jellybeans were colored; in the one on the right, only 9% were. But people still preferred to pick from the bowl that they "knew" had lower odds of success, because they "felt" it offered more ways to win (Zweig, *Your Money & Your Brain* [New York: Simon & Schuster, 2007], 21).

**10% red**

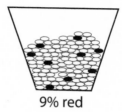
**9% red**

Let's try this: If the stock market dropped 30 percent in one day, and all the "financial experts" were on TV saying this is the greatest buying opportunity ever experienced, would you:

**a.** Buy low (on the dip)
**b.** Sell for fear of what the future may bring

When the market drops considerably, many of my clients will call. Some will call and say, "Are we buying? This is the greatest opportunity since Dell went public!" Others call to say, "This is scary. With inflation and higher taxes, things are going to get worse—much worse. Should we sell today?"

Neither set of callers knows what will happen. Don't misunderstand; neither do I—nor do I care to debate a subject that is predominately random. As you will learn, I only care about my system and the probabilities my system creates for success (I only need the probabilities slightly favorable to stack in my favor). But both talk with conviction. Both are decisive. In fact, this is what makes a market—a buyer and a seller.

Chances are if I am on TV (as a commentator or guest of a financial show) on a day the market drops dramatically and argue that this market action creates a great buy, you would buy. If I argue that Armageddon is upon us, you would sell. I appeal to your brain, the reflective brain that makes intuitive, quick decisions. Although this part of the brain has many components, the brain still acts irrationally and often makes impulsive decisions.

I believe that most often, when you make an attempt at a rational analytical decision, it is really your intuitive or reflexive brain that is making that decision.

## IRRATIONAL POUNCING IS QUITE RATIONAL AND PROFITABLE

Like I said, it is not your fault, it is how our brains are wired to fight or flee. The human brain is wired for survival and pleasure seeking. One component of the Pounce Platform seeks to discover aggressive investments at the height of a recession. Sounds counterintuitive, possibly illogical and aggressive, but my system is the exact opposite of illogical. In fact, it is lower-risk, as measured by many risk measurements, and it is potentially quite profitable. To engage in a strategy of this nature, however, requires a specific system. Left alone, our brains will fight hard to override our thoughts—thinking they are saving us from ourselves.

After Pearl Harbor, during the Bay of Pigs, after President Kennedy's assassination, after 9/11, or during the 2001–2002 recession—in any of these instances, intuition tells you to run from a burning building—from stocks that may go lower due to a hurricane on terrorist attack. After all of these events the market rebounded, making each of these situations a "good buy." If you would have invested right before these seemingly random occurrences, and allowed your intuitive brain to talk you into selling right after, you would have been (are?) still kicking yourself.

## NEWS FLASH

As I write in November 2008, the market is currently in one of the worst bear markets ever recorded, and just completed one of the worst Octobers on record.

This is a pouncing opportunity of epic proportions. Follow the lessons taught within these pages. Wait for the confirmation that a trend has developed. Heed what the investment strategies reveal and pounce away.

## MEN VS. WOMEN—VASTLY DIFFERENT INVESTORS

Who are the better investors, men or women? No, I am not sexist, and this is not a race. The fact is, men's and women's differences extend into the way each group approaches investing. Perhaps it's encoded in our DNA sequences?

**Quiz Yourself. Circle your best answer.**

| | | |
|---|---|---|
| Who takes more risk? | Men | Women |
| Who does more research? | Men | Women |
| Who has a higher rate of error? | Men | Women |
| Who is more knowledgeable? | Men | Women |
| Who is the more confident investor? | Men | Women |
| Who has a superior investment return? | Men | Women |

✓ Men take more risks in investing and are more likely to put too much money into one investment.

✓ Women do more research; women are more cautious investors and are less likely to buy a hot investment without doing research.

✓ Men tend to have a higher rate of error in investing. Women are more likely to sell a winning investment more quickly, while men often wait too long and are less likely to repeat the same mistake twice.

✓ Women are more knowledgeable investors than men.

✓ Women report they are less knowledgeable about investing than men, but in fact they are more knowledgeable—they just enjoy it less than men.

✓ When asked whether emotions played a role in investment mistakes, men are more likely to cite greed (32 percent of men vs. 15 percent of women), overconfidence (33 percent vs. 20 percent), and impatience (28 percent vs. 19 percent).

✓ Women describe themselves as successful investors more often than men do.

✓ Men are much more confident investors.

✓ Women are superior investors—when they have invested. However, the brokerage returns sampled of the Merrill Lynch study (see below) show that the statements of accounts owned by men did better because they invest more often, whereas women are more often in money markets.

This is truly fascinating: A groundbreaking survey of investors by Merrill Lynch Investment Managers found that women make fewer investment mistakes than men and make them less often. Despite this fact, on average women tend to know less of investing and enjoy investing less.

What's the takeaway—that men pounce more than women? That is no surprise.

The facts are: Men take more risks, operate on hot tips, study less, trade more, require less detail, and are more confident. Men have a tendency to be more aggressive, and women err on the side of caution.

## FACE THE FACTS OF LIFE!

Face the facts: I just stated that men trade more than women. Men tend to buy and sell randomly, with a view to short-term wins and lack of strategy—not long-term investing. We know that is just wrong behavior.

Although the data show that women who do invest do better, overall men invest more, so their returns (as measured by a sampling of overall portfolio growth) are still higher than those of women. This is not because they are better investors, but because they do it more. I have no doubt that if women engaged in the practice more frequently, they would outstrip men as better investors.

I once learned that a hastily executed plan that is in motion is better than a well-laid-out plan that is never executed. I think the same holds true here—you've got to pounce to get any action!

But the real takeaway is the realization of how perfect this discovery is. Men and women DO make terrific partners. So, men, put away your ego, do what you are doing, but allow a woman to help you, teach you. Or, simply, truly find a female partner when it comes to researching, investing, and creating strategy.

## SO WHAT DO WE DO WITH OUR BRAIN?

I created the Pounce Platform to help nullify the effects of your brain. My system is predominantly objective. You gather the data included in the P3 indicators. The outcome will help reveal the direction of the market. Based on this you will create your Personal Pounce Platform incorporating the proper investment strategies included in Book Three. These strategies provide a specific screening process for buying and selling.

Some of you will still attempt to add your own flavor, your secret sauce, if you will. I don't necessarily blame you. But, to be sure to utilize both sides of your brain, create a checklist and a system. Remember to ask yourself questions that flush out useless noise to get to the core of the decision.

### Pre-Investment Checklist

1. Does the proposed investment have more upside than downside risk?
2. Does the investment fit my Personal Pounce Platform?
3. Be careful of being hypnotized by fancy brochures, letters,

or annual reports. Try to determine what these reports are selling and what they are not telling you. What does not make sense?

4. Always be skeptical. Ask why.
5. What is your plan? If you are wrong, when do you sell? If you are right, when do you sell?
6. Never make an impulsive move, no matter how "urgent" the decision is. Sleep on the decision; after all, you are king of the jungle.
7. Always try to stick to your platform, allowing the minimum number of subjective decisions in your thought process.

## SUMMARY

You have always known when something was a bit off. Your instinct was great, but eventually something snagged you. It was your intuition foreclosing on your analytical brain.

People make markets. People overdo it on the way up, and overdo it on the way down. All you need to do is look down upon your kingdom, watch the direction of the herd, pounce down, get some lunch, and pounce back up. But the key to success? Rely on your systems. Be true and disciplined to your strategy, and greatness will be yours.

## BOOK TWO

# AIM

## Master Your P3 Indicators

**BOOK ONE HAS MADE** you aware that it is more important to have a system than it is to "go with your gut." Our brains usually prompt us to do the wrong thing at the wrong time. The more structure we create, the better the chance of success.

Using our P3 indicators we will look to determine the value and direction of the market. Not that it changes ANY of the investment systems that you incorporate into your Personal Pounce Platform. But by understanding where the market is going, you will be better equipped to decide which investment strategies to use within your Personal Pounce Platform.

Then we will begin to explore various markets, such as the bull and the bear. Regardless of what you have been told, every bull and bear market cycle is prompted by and begins for different reasons and ends for different reasons. Sometimes fear will create a bear market; sometimes a bear market is created because investments are too expensive. Sometimes bull markets begin because of new technology, sometimes because of the economy. You must know that there is no constant as to which sectors and stocks will outperform. After testing and retesting everything, what I found is that we will never know precisely what causes these markets to begin and end. However, the perfect combination measuring specific valuation criteria against the economic trend and Investor Psyche/Market Behavior will reveal with enough certainty what point of the economic cycle we are in. With this information you will pull out, like arrows from your quiver, the proper investment strategies to include in your Personal Pounce Platform.

# 4

# The Power of Three

Have you ever noticed how frequently the number three seems to pop up in life? I notice it whenever I talk to my kids (three strikes); when I make a presentation (opening statement, salient points, closing); when I consider events that happen in my life; and even when I write a letter. Letters have an opening paragraph, body, and closing paragraph: three pieces—nice and neat.

In life, the Power of Three makes even more sense. In psychology, Freud proposed that the psyche was divided into three parts: the ego, superego, and id. Did you also realize three is a lucky number in Chinese culture? Three is lucky because the word *three* sounds like the word for *alive*, whereas the word *four* sounds like the word *death* in the Chinese language. Perfect music is created in a jazz trio (this of course is a fact, not an opinion). Plato described a perfect society to include three groups: laborers, warriors (or guardians), and rulers (or philosophers).

So, although you have a right to be skeptical, I can deliver a superior investment system using three simple indicators. These tools will act as a guide to determining the direction of the market. These indicators are code-named Power 3 (affectionately, P3).

Once market direction is decided upon, we will determine which investment strategy to utilize within your personal investment platform. We will create a unique investment platform designed using the P3 indicators. From here forward this investment platform will be known as your Personal Pounce Platform.

Please don't confuse the P3 indicators, which are three tools designed to determine market direction, with your Personal Pounce Platform. The Personal Pounce Platform is your investment model. However, based on the outcome of the P3 indicators, your dynamic Personal Pounce Platform will be modified.

## HOW REFRESHING

Never again do you have to chase a hot stock or worry if you are in the right investments. You'll have no need to be afraid of bubbles (I'll talk about taking advantage of bubbles later) or question what you should do during a bear or bull market.

The P3 indicators guide you as to the direction of the market. You will determine a bull, bear, or neutral market reading. Do I claim it will be 100 percent accurate? No, of course not! P3 is not designed for this. It is designed to create an abundance of evidence that will objectively allow you to determine market direction.

With this knowledge, your Personal Pounce Platform will become bullish, bearish, or neutral. Subjectivity is minimized and objectivity is maximized. It is proactivity at its best, as opposed to reactivity at its worst.

## IS IT THAT IMPORTANT TO KNOW THE DIRECTION OF THE MARKET?

Good question. And, yes, it is. As you read you will become as familiar with market cycles such as bull and bear markets as hunters are with their prey. A strange, almost intimate, bond will be formed.

### P3 Revealed

1. Value
2. Economic Direction
3. Investor Psyche/Market Behavior

*Value*

Markets move from fair value to overvalued and back to undervalued. Fair value is a bit subjective but would usually mean a stock is trading in the middle of its valuation range.

As stocks move higher and lower valuation measures such as price to sales, price to cash flow, and price to earnings move higher and lower. Middle range, assuming that earnings and sales show nothing out of the ordinary, is usually fair value. If the stock trades in the middle of the trading range but announces a few new contracts and next year earnings and sales will be substantially higher than projected, would be cause for the stock to be considered undervalued.

The salient point for the Pounce investor is fair value is different for *us* than it is for *them*. Most investors are trying to value a company and determine fair value based on the value they feel the company is worth should they wish to buy the entire company.

Meaning they are often trying to find the private equity value of the company. This is not the objective of the Pounce investor. Our objective is to buy stocks we think are going to go up in price. Many stocks we buy might be considered fair value in the traditional sense, but many will be considered overpriced. Pounce investors are focused on what makes stocks go higher, not the private equity value of the company. And although price to sales and price to earnings are good valuation measures and should be part of our valuation "brew," they are not all that should be considered when a stock goes higher.

The Pounce system does not ask you to trade daily—we are directed to look at our investments and trade once per month, at most. However, we do trade much more than the traditional buy-and-hold investor. As a result, I am not overly concerned if I feel a company is undervalued now based on a twenty-year valuation. I care about what is important in terms of valuation to make my stock go up (if I am long), or go down (if I am short).

There are many elaborate systems, and I applaud the system creators for their efforts, designed to show you cheap stocks, value stocks, stocks going higher, and others. Ignore all of these systems and remember that your sole responsibility is to use the preponderance of evidence to determine if the company is undervalued or overvalued *for purposes of stock appreciation*. Period. There is not just one indicator or strategy that will help with this. Stating that a company growing its earnings is trading at a low price-to-earnings ratio, for example, will not produce a meaningful system that will allow you to build a winning investment model. However, several tested indicators used together will. The collective evidence you gather will give you the necessary information needed to be right more often than not with regard to valuation.

With regard to the P3 indicators, everything compares to

value. Value is compared to the economy. Value is compared to Investment Psyche/Market Behavior. If valuation is high (which is negative), you would need both other indicators positive in order to be slightly bullish. If valuation is low, only one other indicator would allow you to be bullish.

## Economic Direction

It is simple. The economy will grow and eventually overheat. At about the time everyone is on board, believing that this ship (our economic growth) can't sink, it will. A different reason, a different trigger, will always cause the ship to sink, but sink it most certainly will. When the economy falters, it happens fairly rapidly. While every contraction is different, the preponderance of evidence will be present. By the time a recession is actually identified, at least formally, it will most likely be at the tail end of the decline, and stocks likely soon trend higher. Relying on any entity to tell you where the economy is will not be very helpful. However, you will know that when all is felt to be lost, and the absence of any positive news is the norm, a new expansion will reemerge. For some strange reason it will surprise everyone that the economy is actually back in good spirits.

## Investor Psyche/Market Behavior

Finally, as I've said several times, it is all about people. People create markets. You could have the greatest value in the worst economy (a good thing), but if nobody will buy the investment, it can't go higher (which is why we track Investment Psyche/Market Behavior). People create overvalued and undervalued situations—and people are usually wrong. Which is why I often say investing is counterintuitive. Using intuition to invest is usually not a profitable strategy.

## THE P3 KEY

| Valuation | Economy | Psyche | Key |
|---|---|---|---|
| | Bearish | Bearish | Bearish |
| | Neutral | Bearish | Bullish |
| | Bullish | Bearish | Bullish |
| | Bearish | Neutral | Bullish |
| **Extremely Bullish** | Bearish | Bullish | Bullish |
| | Neutral | Neutral | Bullish |
| | Neutral | Bullish | Bullish |
| | Bullish | Neutral | Bullish |
| | Bullish | Bullish | Bullish |
| | | | |
| | Bearish | Bearish | Bearish |
| | Neutral | Bearish | Neutral |
| | Bullish | Bearish | Bullish |
| | Bearish | Neutral | Neutral |
| **Bullish** | Bearish | Bullish | Bullish |
| | Neutral | Neutral | Bullish |
| | Neutral | Bullish | Bullish |
| | Bullish | Neutral | Bullish |
| | Bullish | Bullish | Bullish |
| | | | |
| | Bearish | Bearish | Bearish |
| | Neutral | Bearish | Bearish |
| | Bullish | Bearish | Neutral |
| | Bearish | Neutral | Bearish |
| **Neutral** | Bearish | Bullish | Neutral |
| | Neutral | Neutral | Neutral |
| | Neutral | Bullish | Bullish |
| | Bullish | Neutral | Bullish |
| | Bullish | Bullish | Bullish |
| | | | |
| | Bearish | Bearish | Bearish |
| | Neutral | Bearish | Bearish |
| **Bearish** | Bullish | Bearish | Bearish |
| | Bearish | Neutral | Bearish |
| | Bearish | Bullish | Bearish |

| Valuation | Economy | Psyche | Key |
|---|---|---|---|
| | Neutral | Neutral | Bearish |
| | Neutral | Bullish | Neutral |
| | Bullish | Neutral | Neutral |
| | Bullish | Bullish | Bullish |
| | Bearish | Bearish | Bearish |
| | Neutral | Bearish | Bearish |
| | Bullish | Bearish | Bearish |
| | Bearish | Neutral | Bearish |
| **Extremely Bearish** | Bearish | Bullish | Bearish |
| | Neutral | Neutral | Bearish |
| | Neutral | Bullish | Bearish |
| | Bullish | Neutral | Bearish |
| | Bullish | Bullish | Bullish |

Use the data that the people give you to determine what they are doing. Since people are usually wrong at the extreme, pivotal moment, this is a dream indicator. If *everyone* is doing one thing, do the opposite.

You will have much ebb and flow based on the direction of the economy, meaning your indicators are dynamic and will change. I am absolutely against buy-and-hold investing. I want to feel comfortable with the trend of the market. If I believe it is moving higher, I will invest accordingly. If it is trending lower, I want to invest accordingly. I believe different criteria are important and should be utilized during each market cycle.

## ANOTHER UPSETTING (NOT QUITE TRAGIC) STORY

During a meeting at work, one young new portfolio manager stated that he was worried about the market and thought bad things were on the horizon.

I was shocked at the statement. Actually, I had to sit down and collect myself. Do I fire this kid? Are we not teaching our principles properly? I responded a bit more harshly than when I get this question from someone in the audience during a speech.

I told him that while I pay him to think, the thinking he needs to do is solely based on how to implement or improve upon our systems. Our systems are what make us shine, not our personal hunches, if the market, or a stock, is moving higher or lower. When there is a meaningful change to measure, the system will alert us and we will react accordingly. My young employee's worry regarding the market is, as we now know, his overeager intuition—trying to help him survive.

## ASK WHY

It is a fair question, is it not? Why do markets cycle from bull to bear and back again? Is it based on the growth of the companies, or lack thereof? Is it based on investors and the people's moods? Or, perhaps these cycles are caused by the economy? I think market cycles are caused by all three of these forces.

If you had a preponderance of evidence that helped you ascertain the direction of the market, would that not be invaluable? Yes. And I think it possible to make a market determination with three simple indicators.

Further, if the markets were moving higher, you could conceivably invest during this phase—running with the bulls—and seek to create a system that strives to find superior investments during the bull market. The classic mistake is not getting out before the market falls. A strategy then must be created to be sure to get out before the market turns, as it always will. Finally, once you do get out, what's next? Do you bet on the down cycle, find a new cycle that you think is going higher, or simply wait in cash until you feel the market will trend higher once again? All three are viable ideas, but they should only be explored if you have an investment strategy and a model to follow—one with prudent risk/reward levels to exploit each of these variables. This is the model you can and will create.

## SUMMARY; AND, A WORD OF CAUTION

Great systems are designed to simply use probabilities in your favor. Through repetition and time, the goal is to design a system that allows you to be right more often than you are wrong and by a wider margin. This book is not a get-rich-quick scheme. Nor is any indicator 100 percent accurate.

In fact, even if you had the best of the best managing your money—a mutual fund, hedge fund, or any other audited investment—I doubt the return would be in excess of 20 percent per year over the last ten years. And this is the best of the best! If they were this good, I think the fund would probably be closed to new investors with anything less than millions to get in.

I have read wonderful academic systems. I have studied mathematically based and fuzzy-logic-based investment strategies. Top down, bottom up, low value, high momentum, etc. I have read many newsletter advertisements and software advertisements about how high these systems' incredible returns are. It is just not reality. Please don't buy into it.

And if it were reality, I am just too darn lazy for that! I don't want to sit and pore over charts every night—charts that probably will not make me a better investor anyhow!

I like having a monthly meeting (even if it is with myself—my two brains meet to go over data and come to an agreement) to review the investment platform, make buy-and-sell decisions, and move on. That is essentially what the Pounce system is. Furthermore, I find that a lot of information you read is just going to cause you to go crazy with the conflicting data and suggestions. Truthfully, all of these activities are reaction-driven.

Please use Pounce as it was intended: as a superior investment model to create superior investment results over time. I believe buying and holding investments is not a superior model, and I believe it to be inefficient. However, Pounce is not a short-term trading model. It is not designed to be abandoned for a new system in a few years. It will have periods of underperformance and loss. Over time, however, the probabilities will be in your favor, you will have built a better mousetrap, and you will be doing better than 99 percent of those investing (at least those that I know).

# 5

## P3: Valuation

### CHAPTER NOTES

1. Valuation matters. Most investors are not successful identifying which measures are important for investment success. Valuation allows you to worry less about noise—the seemingly related but truly irrelevant factors. Valuation is the great equalizer. Regardless of booms or busts; regardless of random events; it is valuation that will ultimately drive performance. Low valuation drives a stock to the upside, high valuation drives it to the downside.

2. Pounce investors realize that valuation techniques vary, depending on whether we are focused, for example on stock appreciation or buying a company. And although investing is, in effect buying a company, we are focused on what drives a stock higher, rather than the private equity value of the company.

3. Think of valuation in terms of the market in the aggregate, first; sectors and industries, second; individual investments, third.

4. What matters the most in terms of valuation is to use the same valuation measures consistently. Those who jump around will become prey.

5. Although this is slightly modified for each market cycle, my predatory instincts primarily focus on earnings per share (EPS) estimates created by the analyst community, and a company's likelihood to meet, exceed, or miss these estimates. It is more important that a company exceed projected increases and continue to increase positive estimates than it is to achieve extremely high growth rates. Sniff out those companies that have superior sales, earnings, and cash flow (SEC) as measured against companies' historic growth rates, or above either the sector or a broad benchmark such as the S&P. Ideally, the growth is absolute and independent of the benchmark. The company should increase earnings and sales regardless of whether the index is dropping.

6. Overpaying for this growth, as you often should and will, will eventually bite you if you stay too long. Although it may be warranted to overpay, just remember a good predator knows when to leave a little meat on the bones and get out before a storm comes.

7. Don't bet an investment bubble is ready to burst or short an expensive company (industrial or sector) on valuation alone. Investor stupidity can artificially support a company for a long time.

8. Regarding P3 indicators, we compare valuation to economy and Investment Psyche/Market Behavior. We never look at economy and Investment Psyche to form a trend without valuation.

9. Cheap companies can remain cheap without positive Investor Psyche and Market Behavior. So don't bother investing just because they are cheap—you will be stuck with dead money.

## THERE IS VALUATION AND THEN EVERYTHING ELSE

Read this chapter for knowledge and education, but realize you will still be able to implement your Pounce Platform just by understanding the theory included in this chapter. You can drive a car without knowing how the engine works, or you can choose to learn about and understand the theory behind the engine. Most of us get by fine driving without knowing the basics of engine maintenance, or how to repair a tire. Most of the time this is fine, but . . .

The investment strategies in Book Three factor everything important about valuation into our screening process. Conceivably you could skip to Book Three, complete the exercises, choose your investment strategies, and build your Personal Pounce Platform. But would it not be better to have a bit of theory? This valuation chapter accomplishes two tasks. First, valuation is the first of the P3 indicators and the one the other two compare against. If valuation is trending lower, on a market-wide level, this is significant and important information for the Pounce investor. If this is true and both other P3 indicators (Economic Direction and Investor Psyche) are also neutral to trending lower, you will change the outlook of your Personal Pounce Platform.

This chapter also tells you what you truly need to know about why stocks rise and fall.

## WHAT'S IT WORTH TO YOU?

Marie, Rose, and Tori were three well-educated women searching for their next business. Rose was out of money and she needed to go back and get a full-time job. Marie and Tori talked to Ellie—Marie's really creative older sister—about what she thought. "A bakery," Ellie said. "You guys are awesome bakers. I know everyone in town and can get us as much catering business as we need. But I think we should buy an existing bakery."

They found one selling for $1,000,000. Should they pay that much for the business? Obviously, it all depends on what the business earns and what it is projected to earn in the future.

If the bakery was already earning $100,000 a year and you assumed future earnings of the same, you would, in effect, pay 10 times earnings for that bakery—a P/E ratio of 10. Price of the business = $1,000,000 divided by $100,000 minus the earnings. Is it worth this price? Isn't that subject to what someone is willing to pay?

Should this be true, then that is how we are going to go about valuing stocks—based on what they are worth to you, me, us: the people.

Have you ever bought a house? What determined the value? Did you look at comparable homes and their selling price? If those other homes sold at lower prices, what would motivate you to pay more? Did you like the color of the paint? How about the kitchen or the beautiful waterfall shower in the master bath? See, value is far more than just historic pricing levels. Your mood and psyche play roles as well.

Now you understand why all three Power indicators—economy, valuation, and Investor Psyche/Market Behavior—must be measured together. Homes, like other investments, are loosely valued based on certain measurements. Homes usually "trade" in a price range in relation to collective income levels. When the homes get expensive and the cost is high compared to income levels, the price will usually contract, or income levels rise, to bring the value in line with historic levels. So the right price isn't really the value, is it? It is what somebody is willing to pay for it—cool, huh?

## History Lesson

The most important rule for valuing stocks, sectors, or the markets as a whole is to be consistent with the tools you use (I repeat this mantra often). If all you do is buy low P/E stocks, don't deviate. If all you do is buy stocks with high earnings, don't deviate. And, to be sure you understand I am not contradicting myself, my theory subscribes to both; hence the importance of P3 market direction indicators.

The historical performance of the stock market would show the average price-to-earnings ratio at something around 15 times earnings. This would change depending on how far back you calculate, and how you calculate earnings. I'll just use 15.

The price-to-sales ratio compares the price of a stock to the company's sales for the year. If a company's sales were $200 billion and, based on its current price, it has a market value (also called market capitalization) of $200 billion, the price-to-sales ratio would be 1.

Deep value investors have argued for years that stocks, even at current valuations, are overvalued. And until they actually fall *below* historical averages (for a minimum of five to as much as twenty years) a bull market cannot begin anew. They may be right—who am I to say? In fact, I tend to *think* that is right. However, if you had not invested during overvalued periods, you'd have missed some of the strongest gains realized during the late 1990s. This is also true for the strong bull market in 2003.

What is the point? If all you use is historical value, you are not valuing stocks to position you to Pounce. You may be establishing a great long-term investment strategy, and, should this be so, my advice is to stick with it and hold on. It's not my way. As I state often and loudly, I believe buy-and-hold investors are going to be deeply upset at their portfolio returns over the next ten years.

I could argue that for a long-term buy-and-hold investor, valuation is really "it." Who cares about the economy, or market behavior—or esoteric concepts such as volume indicators?

As opposed to buy-and-hold forever, how about this as a sample, simple alternate plan? When stocks are undervalued, you buy. When they morph to overvalued, you sell. When they are grossly, maniacally overvalued, you bet they will go down.

This is a fine plan, but the flaw is, valuation, in and of itself, valuation does not drive the market. It is almost to be used as a coincident indicator, if you consider a stock over- or undervalued relying solely on price to earnings, or cash flow, or return on equity. The Pounce investor believes value is created by creating the perfect mix of indicators that drive stocks higher. And, yes, I believe I have a pretty darn good cocktail!

Before we share this cocktail (partly contained in this chapter, but fully revealed in the investment strategies of Book Three), I need to remind you that even if my valuation methodology is near perfect, your investment platform is made better by knowing the trend of the market. To this, the Economic Direction and Investor Psyche must be folded into the equation to truly get a clearer picture.

If a stock is trading at 20 times earnings, it is considered expensive, but if that company grows its earnings next year enough to reduce the P/E to, say, 10 times earnings (assuming no movement in stock price), then one would argue the company may not necessarily be expensive.

To truly understand value, we need to focus just a bit more on a few key valuation measures. We need to look at the value compared to the long-term growth, value compared to the sector, value compared to the market. This allows us to better understand if the company is truly undervalued or overvalued.

Next, we look at the sales and earnings trends. Does the company achieve what the collective analyst estimates are? Does it exceed the estimates?

Finally, we need to bring in P3 Economic Direction and Investor Psyche indicators. Are the indicators trending higher or lower? If the trends are higher, we are more confident regarding the ability for this company to meet its earnings targets. Based on this information, I am more comfortable with the valuation that the market has awarded the stock, regardless if it skews high. However, if the indicators are aggressive and I believe a peak is occurring, or trending lower, I am not comfortable with high valuation. Nor am I comfortable with a lower valuation if the indicators are going lower, unless we are pouncing down by going short, as allowed through our Personal Pounce Platform.

Again, think about the takeaway—although stocks will trend from low valuation to high valuation levels, this is not necessarily what drives the market.

I have expressed my belief that much of the short-term success or failure of a particular investment is random. There is one constant, however. All the randomness in the short term caused by herds, bubbles, psychology, inflation, etc., is leveled, ultimately, by valuation.

As nice as this is to know, the point is, we are looking for absolute wealth, and not all of us have only a long-term platform. This rule also does not help much for bear markets (maybe you lose less), or for the Void markets. Remember, absolute wealth is about realizing positive returns year after year.

## A Quick Word for You Overachievers

When you study the valuation methods in this chapter, you may think I was remiss to exclude a certain valuation method, or not to include a certain combination. Or perhaps I should have used a three-year average P/E vs. a current P/E; or operating earnings vs. nonoperating earnings. If this is *what you are thinking*, you failed to see the point. The only consistent method is sticking to whatever method you are using. So if you are currently going through all that trouble and all the work of complicated analysis, I highly doubt your alpha (the higher the alpha, the better the fund manager performed compared to the benchmark) will be much higher than mine—and this type of analysis takes a great deal of time! Think of a squirrel always running around, gathering acorns. The lion doesn't seem to work that hard for food, yet seems quite content. The squirrel gets pounced.

## VALUE THE MARKET FIRST

First, we will explore the markets and how to value the great beast, and then we will drill down and tackle individual sectors and securities.

We start with markets because the type of market we are in and moving toward will dictate the tone and style of investment.

I recently came across a very popular and interesting graph. Envision a graph showing the markets moving even higher. Brokerage firms send them out any day. This hypothetical graph shows the P/E ratio at 16.5 percent. Further, this graph states: "Surprisingly, stocks are 35% 'cheaper' following a 70% run in stock prices (88% including dividends)."

And you wonder why investors lose money?

First of all, the date used is March (3/2000–3/2008). This is the first hint. Of course the number is not arbitrary; they knew that March was the market peak. And, yes, the market should peak at 30 times earnings. Any market that trades double the historic average is too expensive based on current earnings. More importantly, however, the earnings growth for that same period is and was in no way sustainable. One valuable lesson you will need to embrace involves "expected earnings." It is my experience that when "the good times are rolling," analysts are way too optimistic with earnings projections (amazing all that money spent at Harvard and they still let their greedy brains get in the way of sound analysis). And when the earnings are bad, or the economy is weak, the projected earnings are often wildly understated. Thus you see many companies exceed analysts' expectations when earnings are depressed—leading to stock gains. And, when earnings are optimistic and the stock rises at a faster rate than earnings, the stocks often miss analyst expectations and subsequently fall back to earth. When the market or sector has been experiencing accelerating earnings, discount the growth that the analysts feel is the true potential of the company. And when earnings are depressed, use the analysts' expectation. (Knowing they are probably understated.) What you are looking for is a company that still has greater upside potential than downside risk.

The second problem with this hypothetical graph is: In March 2008 the P/E was low based on current earnings, but the economic slowdown was evident, which would affect earnings, which would drive the P/E higher unless stocks dropped.

Finally, and this should make lots of sense—16 times earnings still isn't cheap!

## NEWS FLASH

Think back to the middle of 2007. The stock market was in a strong rally mode, and had been for a few years. After the 2002 recession stocks went from cheap (or fair valued) to expensive based on historical metrics. Analysts argued that earnings and sales in the new "global economy" would continue to rise at a rate that justified the higher multiples of stocks. Think back to the mood of the people. China would grow forever. U.S. stocks were strong. Interest rates were low. People felt great. It took just a few short months for the mood to go from overly optimistic, to extremely pessimistic. Doom and gloom abounded. The stocks anticipating the worst sold off to what I believe to be a long-term undervalued level.

As I write, stocks are at a very low point and the mood of the world is just as low. Fears of a total credit crisis and a major depression are daily topics of conversation. So let me write the next chapter (of the world events) before it happens; the economy will go into a recession. The stock market anticipating this will begin to rise before the economy does. Slowly but surely the economy will once again rise, the housing market will stabilize and jobless numbers will once again come down. We will begin to fear inflation and other unforeseen issues, as the recession recesses further back in our minds.

## Can You Pounce Using P/E Ratios?

We discussed P/E ratios several times in *Pounce* as it is a very common, and important tool. Price to earnings is an important tool if used properly, but *only* in conjunction with a few other key indicators. Price to sales, the seemingly forgotten little brother, is one of these key indicators the Pounce investor uses. The other is earnings revisions and earning expectations.

When testing the variables to see what works, you want to find a pattern. Most of what is thought to be a pattern is not. Stocks rally during periods of economic growth, during higher and lower interest, during high and low inflation. Stocks can also drop during those same periods. So to use generalizations to determine where the market is at is a waste of time.

One truth does remain. When stocks begin to sell off, they tend to go from neutral (fair value) to undervalued. When stocks trend from neutral higher, they will stretch to aggressive overvalued levels. Stocks will remain overvalued until a trend of catalysts causes the herd to leave. Some of these catalysts will include a deceleration of earnings and sales. Others will include the consumer mood (Investor Psyche) as well as the economic trend. Regardless of the initial trigger, the collective trend is what will ultimately create a "reversion of the mean," causing multiples to compress and pushing stocks down.

Once stocks, sectors, or markets trade at excessive valuations, it is more difficult for stocks to continue to rise. The reward/risk ratio is reversed. There is greater chance of a stock dropping as opposed to rising further. Either it is virtually impossible to keep growing earnings or sales at the same momentum levels or earnings and sales will fall if the consumer slows down and takes the economy with it. Or, earnings will slow because people will be afraid of earnings and sales falling, causing investor psychology and market action to turn negative. The herd runs in another direction, and the stock will eventually drop. Like the economic cycle, it is a continuous loop. A never-ending loop.

On average, the stocks with low price to earnings will perform better over time. However, the long-term return of a value stock and that of a growth stock is about the same. It is a classic case of a reversion to the mean. When growth gets too expensive, money goes to value; when value is too expensive, growth should be cheap. When large companies are too expensive, chances are (for a variety of reasons) small is cheap. You get the picture.

Many analysts argue that a true long-term secular bull market (think 1990s) cannot ever begin and has not ever begun unless a market is cheap. The most popular first screen for determining value (cheap vs. expensive) is price-to-earnings ratio.

I really love this work by Vitaliy Katsenelson for a few of the interesting points it reveals. It reveals that earnings, as we have discussed, do not need to be exceedingly good for a bull market. But if earnings are bad, it is never good. The conclusion—it would be important to measure markets and stocks with bad earnings to either get out of their way or pounce on them. If earnings are good, it is not pouncing time, using earnings growth alone. What the Pounce investor does is takes this concept one step further.

First, we realized that it is not, in fact, the earnings alone that

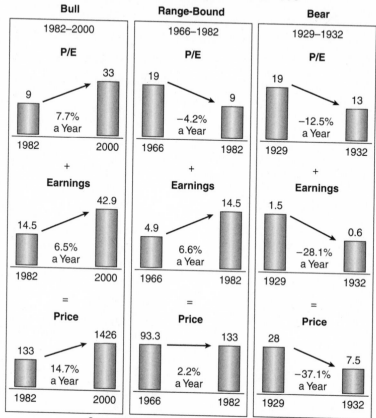

Sources of Price Return of S&P 500

drive stocks. Rather, earnings expectation does. This is an important distinction. You have heard of stocks that have a quarter of 20 percent earnings growth, but the stock gets killed. This is because the expectation was probably above 20 percent. What you can, and we do, track is not earnings specifically but whether or not companies are outperforming what they are expected to earn. Add this to a few other factors, such as price to earnings and dividends, and you will have a tasty, tasty cocktail.

Stocks go from cheap to expensive as compared to P/E and back again.

The average P/E for the market since the early 1900s is roughly 14.5 times earnings. Although the markets may rally at a starting P/E of higher than 15, bull markets need to get cheaper than the average to begin a new bull cycle.

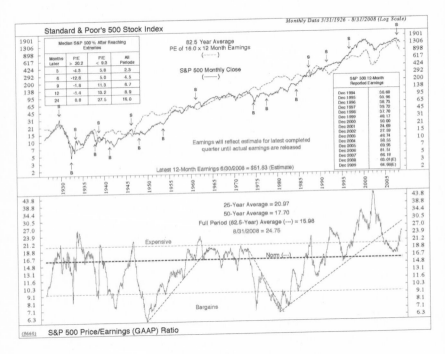

## Flaw in P/E

Price-to-earnings ratio is an important, consistent guide for measuring the current value of the market. It has two (and a half) flaws that an investor must overcome.

Assume I agree that long-term secular bull markets do not begin until stocks are cheap as measured by P/E ratios (under 13 times earnings). Unfortunately, the knowledge would not have made you much money throughout the bull market of the 1990s. By 2001–2002 the bull crashed down, so eventually the markets did fall. Before the bull market petered out in late 2007, an investor enjoyed a great run from late 2002 until the third quarter of 2007. So the first flaw is that P/Es work best to call long-term market direction. This, as you will see, will be important for a specific portion of your Personal Pounce Platform, but it is not your only weapon.

The second problem with price-to-earnings ratio is "E." If you are attempting to project the P/E of a company, say, next year, or for future years in general, earnings are an unknown variable. Analysts that predict future earnings are often incorrect and will often revise their numbers higher and lower. If a company trades at $10 per share and earns $1, it will have a P/E of 10. But what if the economy goes to hell in a handbasket, and the stock of this company drops to $8 while the earnings are horrible, and drop to $0.50? The P/E would be very high at 16. Because the economy is so poor, analysts are expecting the company to earn $0.50 next year. But the economy rebounds and the earnings actually come in at back to their old $1 level. If the stock is still depressed, at $8, the P/E is only 8. Of course, the analysts didn't see the bump in price coming. And if it did happen, the stock would probably have risen, and you would have missed a pouncing opportunity. So the second problem with P/E is the variability in "E."

Which leads to another half of a problem. How do we calculate P/E? Do we use trailing 12, projected next year, current operating earnings, or perhaps an average of a three-year period? I will have some thoughts on this, but suffice it to say that, as with all strategies, the most important thing is to choose criteria and stick to them.

A good rule of thumb would be: Either through continued

average earnings growth (and no stock appreciation—the Void), or through a violent bear market, look for a low P/E.

Why use the three-year average? Because using the one-year average can artificially skew the number. Also, don't use projected earnings if we are in a bull market. Skew the number lower, to avoid a false sense of security that an artificially inflated P/E could give you.

If we are in a bear market, and the indicators show an economy that has bottomed out and is indicating a neutral reading, you should project slightly better earnings numbers.

Further, a general rule is that any time the P/E has reached extremes to the high side, the market has reacted very poorly—regardless of what the fund managers are projecting.

We have established that P/E ratios work for calling secular bear and bull markets. Now what? Other than these extremes, using P/E ratios for calling the direction of market indexes is not the only determining factor. When deciding the direction of markets, use P/E for determining if we are in a secular bear or bull market. P/E must be used with a few other key valuation metrics as well.

## BUILD YOUR P3 VALUATION INDICATOR

To determine a company's value is critical, regardless of whether you invest in individual stocks or exchange traded funds. Don't buy just because something is cheap. Even to check up on your mutual fund, you will want to review the top ten holdings (give or take) to see if you agree with the fund manager's selections. But remember: What is cheap will stay cheap. We care about the trend!

When you create your investment model, the Personal Pounce Platform, it will be modified depending if the P3 indicators say the trend is bullish, bearish, or neutral. Everything compares to valuation. If valuation is bullish, one of the other two factors must confirm this trend. The same is true for bearish, or neutral.

Note that we are valuing markets or individual stocks for investment appreciation potential. Should you be attempting to buy real estate, or a company outright, or buy and hold the company for a long, long time, I would use different models and sets of criteria for evaluation.

A case in point is Warren Buffett's approach to evaluating a company. He looks for both superior value and superior growth. But he values a company based on what he believes is its private equity value. He does not pay much attention to the P/E, or whether the stock is in the top quintile of sales growth. He can buy deeply undervalued companies, and he can afford to wait many years until what he believes to be their value is reflected in their stock price—through appreciation, one hopes.

Many smart people will try to determine intrinsic value or create discounted cash flow models to determine a company's value. This is acceptable for long-term valuation, but will it cause the stock to go higher?

As you will learn in Book Three, I believe that, for a portion of your Personal Pounce Platform, investing in sectors and industries is as beneficial as, if not more beneficial than, investing in individual stocks. When you own sectors, you can enjoy the advantages of being in a class of stocks that is superior based on collective valuations, reduce some of the risk and randomness of investing specifically in one company, and capture much of the upside. When one has the time and funds to invest in individual stocks, I still highly encourage this type of investment prey, but it must be done in the context of your Personal Pounce Platform in order to maximize return and minimize risk.

At the risk of being redundant, let me reemphasize I am not buying these businesses to own forever. Rather, I want to find a company that I think has a better probability of moving higher, by a higher percentage than lower. Knowing that much of the market is "random" in the short term, I will further increase my probabilities by using my chosen system of investing (and remember, the system itself is less important than the fact that you *have* a system) to speculate in several corporations.

What I find is interesting is that many commonalities and definable patterns do exist. Although I do not have the data to go back to every market upturn and downturn, I can with a fair degree of certainty state that:

The stocks moving higher in a down market exceed analysts' estimates. Further, low-beta, income-generating, and low price-to-sales and price-to-earnings stocks tend to outperform the entire index during down markets.

Stocks that move higher in up markets also tend to exceed analysts' estimates. Price to earnings and price to sales matter less, as do the income and beta numbers.

*Scoring Valuation*

The following table might look a bit intimidating, but it is not. I only use three main variables to value the market. That's because valuing the market is not difficult. And it should not simply be based on P/E or P/S. If P/E is low and forecasted earnings are low, that is very bullish to me. If earnings are forecasted higher than historical averages, this is bearish—as it is not sustainable. Much of the work you see in P3 is counterintuitive. We run against the herd—that's why we like bubbles; we are already prepared.

To get the data for individual stocks or sectors, go to a Web

# THE P3 VALUE SCORING CHART

## Price-to-Earnings Ratio

Average P/E assumed to be 15

|  | Price to Earnings |  | Score |
|---|---|---|---|
| **Extremely Overvalued** | P/E ≧ 17.25 | Extremely Bearish | −2 |
| **Overvalued** | 16.5 < P/E ≦ 17.25 | Bearish | −1 |
| **Fair Value** | 13.5 < P/E ≦ 16.5 | Neutral | 0 |
| **Undervalued** | 12.75 < P/E ≦ 13.5 | Bullish | 1 |
| **Extremely Undervalued** | P/E ≦ 12.75 | Extremely Bullish | 2 |

## Price-to-Sales Ratio

Average assumed to be 1.1

|  | Price to Sales |  | Score |
|---|---|---|---|
| **Extremely Overvalued** | P/S > 1.26 | Extremely Bearish | −2 |
| **Overvalued** | 1.21 < P/S ≦ 1.26 | Bearish | −1 |
| **Fair Value** | 1 < P/S ≦ 1 | Neutral | 0 |
| **Undervalued** | 0.9 ≦ P/S ≦ 1 | Bullish | 1 |
| **Extremely Undervalued** | P/S < 0.9 | Extremely Bullish | 2 |

## Earnings Growth

Average Earnings Growth assumed to be 8%

|  | Earnings Growth |  | Score |
|---|---|---|---|
| **Extremely Overvalued** | Forecasted Growth > 9.6% | Extremely Bearish | −2 |
| **Overvalued** | 8.8% ≦ Forecasted Growth ≦ 9.6% | Bearish | −1 |
| **Fair Value** | 7.2% < Forecasted Growth ≦ 8.8% | Neutral | 0 |
| **Undervalued** | 6.6% ≦ Forecasted Growth ≦ 7.2% | Bullish | 1 |
| **Extremely Undervalued** | Forecasted Growth < 6.6% | Extremely Bullish | 2 |

**Scoring Key**
If the score is less than –6, then Extremely Bearish
If the score is between –3 and –6, then Bearish
If the score is between –3 and 3, then Neutral
If the score is between 3 and 6, then Bullish
If the score is above 6, then Extremely Bullish

site such as morningstar.com (which I find very useful). Once on the site, type in any stock symbol. A snapshot will appear. Select valuation ratios. From this point, you should spot a "Forward Valuation" tab. Select this tab, which will give you the Standard & Poor's 500 forward P/E and the PEG (the relationship between the P/E ratio and earnings growth). With this information, simply divide the price by the forward P/E to get the forward four-quarter earning per share estimate.

So all you need to do is plug in the values for any stock, and your score tells you how to look at the value. We'll do similar scoring exercises for Economic Direction and Investor Psyche in the two following chapters.

## ONE MORE GIFT FOR YOU

As I continue to remind you, all the investment screens and parameters have been created for you. Included in Book Three are your investment strategies and how to incorporate these strategies into your Personal Pounce Platform; but you might also want to venture a bit on your own and act independently, within the Pounce guidelines.

To help you on your journey, I have included another valuation cheat sheet of all the important indicators I would use for individual stock valuation. These valuation points are important to help me find stocks that win, not to buy and hold a company that I think might be undervalued.

## Is a Stock Poised to Appreciate?

*Earnings*

A company is measured on both its earnings and the ability to exceed earnings expectations. An accounting discussion is not necessary. What is necessary is to ascertain what drives stocks higher or lower. Stocks that increase their earnings, and continue to revise earnings higher, tend to enjoy superior stock appreciation. This statement is generally true during up and down markets.* Be careful, however: Stocks with torrid earnings growth usually grow more quickly than a reasonable multiple for this earnings growth (P/E and PEG). As much as we want accelerating earnings growth, it is not usually recommended to overpay for this growth or "buy" a stock solely for earnings acceleration—unless this is for the Top Gun portion of your Personal Pounce Platform. Never do so if you do not have a definitive sell discipline.

We receive information on earnings from a few different sources. The first is the company. All companies publish quarterly and annual earnings data. The earnings that they report are one screen that

---

* Ken Stern & Associates has tested stocks within the Standard & Poor's 500 Index using many screens and regressions. In general, companies that exceed analysts' expectations, experience earnings revisions, and provide positive earnings outlooks outperform stocks within the Standard & Poor's 500 Index. This is true over varying time frames, and over varying markets. A few caveats do exist. First, some data is limited during certain date periods. This could alter the information. Second, depending on the screens that call for a monthly, quarterly, or semiannual rebalancing, without rebalancing the portfolio and selling those stocks that do not continue this trend, the results vary dramatically. Third, during several periods, limited stocks actually made the screens, arguing the point that the data may not be statistically significant.

we track. The second screen we track is how far above or below the actual earnings reported were from the analysts' projected earnings. As a community, analysts will estimate what a company's earnings will be for a quarter or for the year. All of the analysis that follows and projects a company's earnings will be compiled and averaged. We often track to see if the company exceeds this average projection or misses this projection. You may hear a news report that states, "Earnings of XYZ failed to meet expectations." This is what is meant by that. Further, we then may track how a stock performs if the company fails to meet or exceed analysts' expectations. Often a company may rally even though they fail to meet the "street's" expectations if the company affirms or states that they are comfortable with current earnings estimates, guidance, the full year guidance, or increases the projections for the next quarter.

This leads to a further set of earnings analysis. Some companies will create their own earnings' projection, and offer their own guidance as to what they believe their earnings will be for the next quarter or the next year. We (Ken Stern & Associates) have found that companies that do offer guidance, that increase their earnings guidance for the next quarter and/or year, tend to outperform the index as a whole.

I understand this discussion on earnings was perhaps more then you bargained for. Please be reminded that you do not have to do the work. Many Web sites that offer stock screening have very good tracking methods. We built the screens for you in Book Three. We did the testing and know how to build these screens.

### Earnings Rules:
1. Steady systematic earnings increases
2. Growth in the percent of earnings

3. Surprise in earnings announcement compared to forecast
4. Positive earnings guidance

*Overachiever: Extra Credit.* Okay, for all you overachievers: You are probably asking if I refer to operating earnings, trailing earnings, forward earnings, or earnings for an average period of time. Just look for the trend and be consistent—you will arrive at the same conclusion no matter which you use.

But if you are an overachiever, then I suggest you take apart the earnings statement and consider the quality of earnings. In a strong bull market, all companies with any earnings will rise. However, many studies and tests prove that stocks with the highest-quality earnings will outperform those with the lowest-quality earnings. Quality can be measured two ways; the first is to take into account one-time or special charges that companies often take to reflect what they consider unusual or one-time events. Layoffs or other restructuring movements would be an example of this. You may argue that the event is truly a one-time event, but, hey, the numbers are the numbers. Add it all in and let the investors decide if they think there will be an upside to your earnings numbers by taking it out.

## Revenue

Earnings are extremely important, of that I have no doubt. What is amazing is how stock investors hardly give revenue (sales) data the time of day. Yet it is arguably just as important as, if not more important than, earnings for a company. And using revenue to help pick winning or losing stocks has been quite successful.

Have you ever considered buying income real estate, such as an apartment building? What was the first question you asked? Probably, What were the gross rents for the building? This is revenue (sales). You probably asked later what the net income or cash flow was.

When buying a business, most people first ask what the sales are, then they ask about income.

The sales a company reports are one of the purest measures of a company's worth. Of course, without earnings, what good are sales? I contend that sales are closer to "pure," whereas earnings (as we just reviewed) are easier to manipulate. Once a certain critical mass is achieved, fixed costs should drop as a percentage, allowing for earnings to expand.

A 2005 paper entitled "Revenue Surprises and Stock Returns," by Narasimhan Jegadeesh and Joshua Livnat, explored revenue and stock prices. The conclusion: "We find significant abnormal returns in the post announcement period for stocks that have large revenue surprises, after controlling for earnings surprises. Although analysts revise their forecasts of future earnings in response to revenue surprises, they are slow to fully incorporate the information in revenue surprises." I could not have said it better.

What I again observe is that regardless of whether we are in an up or down market, stocks that increase their revenue, and surprises to the upside (compared to analysts' forecasts), predict more persistent future earnings growth. Stocks tend to go higher, and the outperformance tends to last for about six months. This could be characterized by stretched valuation metrics (higher P/E multiple, higher P/E sales. Be careful. A stock may outperform the benchmark or compared index but will come down just as hard.

### Revenue Rules:
1. Three-year average revenue growth
2. Revenue accelerating at a faster rate than the benchmark

and/or industry or sector (simply consistent, predicable earnings)

3. Upside guidance and/or surprise

*Overachiever Extra Credit.* I believe that revenues are a quantifiable valuation metric. However, like the case for earnings, revenue is not always what it seems. If a company's revenue is growing, but, say in retail, stores that have been open for a year are declining in revenue, this is a negative. So when you get down to individual analysis, you need to ask if stores opened for at least one year each increased their sales (same store sales comparison) performance. Further, even if gross revenue increases, but the increase falls below what the analysts projected and/or analysts ratchet down estimates for future revenue, this is a very bad development for the company's stock and earnings. On average, lowered guidance portends further lowered guidance and a weak stock six months later.

## Cash Flow

Cash flow is important for numerous reasons. Companies with positive, ascending cash flow are desirable, and hold their value better than companies without it for several reasons. First, companies with positive, increasing cash flow are more desirable as acquisition targets than those without. They are also in a better position to acquire companies (they can absorb an acquisition easier, and it is easier for them to obtain financing). Cash flow is what remains after subtracting (cash) payments from (current) revenue (an accountant may take issue with this oversimplified definition). But truly, cash is a measure of the financial health of a company. Another way to look at cash flow is as equivalent to net profit, plus charge-offs for depreciation, amortization, and other noncash items.

### Cash Flow Rules:

1. Consistent and steady cash flow. Unlike the sales and EPS numbers, I find that a substantial increase in cash flow is not critical. We are not using "cash flow" as other fundamental analysts often do. They use cash flow as an important measure to determine private equity value, or intrinsic value of a company. I use it to help ferret out stocks that may be rising or falling.

2. Make sure cash flow steadily increases, not decreases. It does not matter the rate of increase so long as it's steady.

3. Look at companies that are ranked in the highest quintile as compared to their peer group for cash flow (this will be more important when using this data for investment strategy and model building).

### Net Profit Margins

Chances are you will begin to see a trend. Stocks with solid earnings and increasing cash flow will also be likely to have a solid profit margin, if not an increasing one.

Net profit margin is expressed as a percentage. It is the percent the company actually realizes in profit. Other margins of profitability, such as return on investment (ROI) and return on assets (ROA), might be important when buying a company. But I do not see a direct correlation between these measures and stock trends. Profit margins, increasing ones at that, work just fine. Don't bother with all the other measures.

Companies that have thin profit margins do not realize a

competitive advantage. If business gets tight, they won't have room to cut costs. Regardless of how great a company may be, I stay away from low-margin companies that are not working toward increasing the margins.

My sweet spot is 8–10 percent, but I have a rule not to buy a stock with a margin lower than 2 percent, on average, for over three years. Incidentally, I think of great companies like Costco that are screened out because of this rule. It goes to show you that not any one indicator drives a stock.

### Dividend

As an investor you make money either though the appreciation on the stock price or the income you are paid. The income is expressed in the form of a dividend.

As you will see in when discussing the Pounce for income and growth investment strategy, the dividend can be absolutely important during periods that the market is in a bear or great void cycle. During bull markets, it is not so important. However, when looking at dividends, you are searching for consistency and the payout ratio. A dividend that represents too much of the company's earnings is an accident waiting to happen.

### A Word About Book Value

Book value is a widely used method of valuing the worth of a company. Take the assets and subtract the liabilities and you have the book value. Overachievers wish to reevaluate what an asset really is and how to value it. They feel that real estate or goodwill may be misrepresented and could affect book value.

All of this is important if you are buying a company to own forever. However, as an investment predator, book value doesn't help very much. The one sector in which it is of some meaningful value is financials.

## DOES THE COMPANY OFFER VALUE?

Earnings, sales, and cash flow must be kept in check. Companies that trade on the growth of these measurements alone trade purely on momentum. And while it may be a good ride, the party will eventually end.

### Price to Earnings

Divide P/E by its own growth rate. Since we already discussed price to earnings, we will focus on its great equalizer, price-to-earnings growth (PEG). Would you rather pay 20 times earnings for a stock or 15 times earnings? It depends on the earnings growth. I would, but only if the earnings I was tracking were growing at 20 percent or higher. If a stock has a low PEG rate, regardless of the raw P/E I would believe this to be a much better value than that of low P/E stock with even lower earnings growth numbers.

Of course, I need to remind you that it depends on the earnings we are using. If we are using current earnings to compute PEG, but the forecast is very bleak, therein lies "the rub." So again the same rules apply:

1. Look for consistencies within the analysts' earnings forecasts for the company (compare first-call estimates with the actual announced estimates).
2. If we are in a bull market, then discount the future earnings growth back to historic earnings growth to determine if the

P/E is still expensive. So, as an example, go on to msnmoney
.com. Click on "Financial Results," click on "Key Ratios," and
then click on "10-Year Summary."

3. If we are in a bear market, you must be assured that you have
the highest-quality company. The combination of a company
P/E trading less than next year's forecasts, a P/E lower than
the industry group or market, and an earnings rising faster
than the market is a wonderful cocktail. This combination is
more important than simply stating: a P/E less than 12 times
earnings.

*Price to Sales*

We discussed the importance of tracking companies that steadily
increase sales. This is important. So, too, is the multiple of sales we
pay. Generally, I do not wish to pay a price-to-sales ratio in excess
of 1.5.

By doing it this way, the valuation screen becomes extremely important. In Book Three you will study the Pounce investment strategies that will comprise your Personal Pounce Platform. Let's consider
for a moment the investment strategy called Rising Stars. In this
screen, I do not accept companies with a price to sales of higher than
1.5. In this regard, when valuation is cheap—which often coincides
with negative or neutral economic P3 indicators, and negative or
neutral Investment Psyche P3 indicators—you will have more stocks
that will fit the criteria for Rising Stars. Subsequently, you will have
more stocks to purchase. When valuation is aggressive, and P3 Economic Direction and Investment Psyche indicators are also aggressive, you will have fewer stocks that make your screen. And this is the
magic of your Personal Pounce Platform.

*Price to Sales Tested*

Jim O' Shaughnessy is one financial expert I greatly respect. He has written a few books about his unique approach to investing, and he also manages a successful fund for the Royal Bank of Canada. What Jim does would be hard for the common folk to accomplish, as he actually takes apart the financials to arrive at what he believes is a company's true earnings, cash flow, etc. He then tests and back-tests variables like price to sales. Jim called the price-to-sales (P/S) ratio the king of all factors. Since this is about your predatory skills, and my desire to make you king, let me impart some of his findings to you.

What Jim did is analyze the stocks with the lowest P/S. He took those with the 50 lowest and the 50 highest P/S. He did this for both all stocks in the universe and then those solely in the large stock universe. What he found was that stocks with low P/S vastly out performed the S&P 500 benchmark. He published the results in his book *What Works on Wall Street*. In summary, he proves that from December 31, 1951, through December 31, 2003, stocks with low P/S, beginning with $10,000, grew to $22 million! As a point of comparison, if you had invested $10,000 in the Standard & Poor's 500 Index, it would have grown to $5 million. The strategy performed well over several periods and various intervals. Basically, stocks with the lowest P/S beat the universe 88 percent of all rolling 10-year periods.

## A FEW MORE USEFUL VALUATION TECHNIQUES

1. Read the letter that the chairman or CEO writes on the annual report. I don't read much of the letter, but I do look to see if foolish excuses such as "weather" are made as to why

earnings are not realized. I worry if too many graphs mask the true nature of the report.

2. Look for stock buybacks. Although a stock may initially receive a bit of a bounce if a company announces a stock buyback, often the buybacks are not actually completed. Yet this is the only way to possibly reduce supply—by taking shares out of circulation while at the same time making a statement to the effect that, at least as far as the company believes, there is value in buying the shares. The action of buying shares back should conceptually reduce supply and increase demand.

3. Value Line timeliness rating. Although the exact method as to how the Value Line timeliness ranking is created is a bit of a secret, the method of computation is virtually all objective and not subject to analysts' opinions. We do not think that the ranking includes long-term company trends, earnings, recent earnings/price momentum, earnings surprises, and much more. But, like everything else, I care less about picking it apart and more for the fact that it has been a useful indicator. The idea is to pick the stocks with the highest timeliness ranking and sell those that are worst. "(1)" is the highest ranking; "(5)," the lowest.

4. Morningstar value rating. Similar to the Value Line timeliness ranking, I find the objectivity of the Morningstar value rating to be quite helpful.

5. Read analyst reports. An analyst report will provide great insight into the company and the sector. Please never use this as a reason to buy or sell a company. In fact, do not look at the rating. Analysts' reports are often extremely subjective, and often wrong.

## SUMMARY

There is no one perfect earnings technique when measuring a stock's value. The perfect cocktail blends together the best of the valuation measures into the growth measures. Depending on which investment strategy you utilize, you will run the screens ranging from monthly to annually. If a stock does not make a screen, it is sold. You are an investor, not a trader. However, you love no stock. If it doesn't make the cut, it doesn't deserve your investment.

Finally, when valuing the market as a whole, you will find the market is trending higher, reaching an aggressive peak, trending lower, or sitting on the bottom. You must compare value to the two other power indicators. P3 value will tell you where the market is at. You will need a confirmation of this from one, if not both, of the other two P3 indicators. With this confirmation, you will structure your Personal Pounce Portfolio as bullish, bearish, or neutral.

# 6

## P3: Economic Direction

### CHAPTER NOTES

1. To possess the ability to pounce during all markets, you must understand the Economic Direction.
2. Bull and bear markets can occur during any phase of the economy—including recessions. EVERY economic cycle provides a window of opportunity for the predator to pounce.
3. Every cycle is different. Focus on the data, not your gut. Outsmarting the system is usually you being rationally irrational again. It does not matter if technology is the new revolution, or if terrorists have declared war, or if housing was the reason we averted a nasty recession in 2001—both contributed to the recession in 2008. Although you cannot time a business cycle perfectly, you can accurately follow the trend and use this trend to modify your investment model.
4. The economy should not be used to determine stock prices. Instead, use it to determine which investment strategy to use.

5. Contraction and recessions are great for Pounce investors and are horrible for those buy-and-hold investors who simply enjoy (how you enjoy losing money, I'm not sure) "staying the course." A recession is usually a great time to pounce.

6. Stop looking for absolutes as they relate to specific action items. This will cause you to get burned. An example: The consumer staples sector is usually the best during a recession. This is the wrong focus. The right focus is to figure out which market, which geographic region, and which market cap have the best valuation and the strongest earnings potential.

7. Remember that bear markets and recessions are not one and the same. Although, bear markets do occur during most recessions and these bear markets are more violent and longer than a stand-alone bear market. Without preparing for this, you will get pounced.

8. In relation to the business cycle, the two best times to invest (for return) are from the recession lows through expansion and from the late expansion into the peak.

### P3 POWER INDICATOR: ECONOMIC DIRECTION

The Pounce investor compares the economy to valuation to determine which investment strategy should be used. You need to remember that valuation (valuation uniquely measured by Pounce investors) is the constant. If valuation is in a bullish trend, but the economy is in a bearish trend, you would be neither bullish nor bearish, you would be neutral, unless Investor Psyche/Market Behavior was either bullish or bearish.

Most financial experts will tell you that a strong economy leads to higher stocks, and that most poor or recessionary economies lead to lower stocks. This is not accurate. In fact, many periods that gross domestic product (GDP) is rushing forward provide minimal stock returns. Look at years 1937 through 1950 as an example. Conversely, many periods with weak GDP have been exceptional periods in the stock market. Look at years 1932 through 1937.

What is true is that most recessions create bear markets, or bear markets can trigger recessions.

What about everyone who says stocks do not perform well when interest rates rise? Don't rates often rise as the economy strengthens? How can you make money if the economy is growing *and* interest rates are rising? Isn't it true that interest rates rose several times during the late 1990s as the stock market roared ahead? Of course, the hangover recession that began in 2001 made us pay for that excess return.

Illustrating these concepts is this handy summary that Vitaliy Katsenelson compiled. He compared GDP, earnings, and inflation to the return in the Standard & Poor's 500 during every decade from 1930 to 2000. Whenever I hear market watchers and economists state that the markets will go up or down based on inflation or GDP, it is cause for some amusement. Actually, from this graph, earnings was the best measure to correlate performance and stock price. You will learn that the Pounce investor takes this one step further. Remember, in one stock or sector for multiple years, we get in, take a few bites, and get out. The Pounce investor's somewhat shorter time investment horizon also focuses on earnings, but more importantly earnings trends.

### Returns One Decade at a Time

| Decade | Nominal Gross Domestic Product | Real Gross Domestic Product | S&P 500 EPS | Inflation (Deflation) | S&P Total Return |
|--------|--------|--------|--------|--------|--------|
| 1930–1940 | −1.4% | 0.5% | −5.0% | −1.9% | 0.0% |
| 1940–1950 | 11.2% | 5.9% | 7.7% | 5.0% | 8.9% |
| 1950–1960 | 6.3% | 3.8% | 5.4% | 2.1% | 19.3% |
| 1960–1970 | 6.6% | 4.5% | 5.6% | 1.9% | 7.8% |
| 1970–1980 | 9.7% | 3.2% | 7.9% | 6.3% | 5.8% |
| 1980–1990 | 8.3% | 3.1% | 5.5% | 6.3% | 17.3% |
| 1990–2000 | 5.6% | 3.0% | 7.1% | 3.4% | 18.0% |
| 1930–2000 | 6.7% | 3.5% | 5.2% | 3.3% | 11.0% |

Copyright 2007–2008, Vitally N. Katsenelson

## If Economic Growth Does Not Affect Market Returns, Why Do We Track It?

Most of us do not want to wait ten years to decide if our investment platform is working. During cycles shorter than ten years, the economy affects earnings, projected earnings (which is more important than actual earnings), Investor Psyche, and, yes, markets. Most recessions were led lower by a declining stock market. And most stock markets also experience bear markets during recessions.

When people refer to an economy in a boom or in a recession, they are usually referring to the national average. The Pounce investor looks for those industries, sectors, markets, and geographic regions that offer promise. If the nation is in a recession, does that mean stocks are cheap? If they are cheap, how cheap are they? When growth continues, will these stocks be great buys? Regardless of a poor economy, capital will find a new home. Bubbles will be formed regardless of the cycle. Embrace the cycle and look for opportunity.

## The Economy and Pouncing Thoughts—Follow the Trend

I love the business cycle. Throughout my life, I must've read thousands upon thousands of pages relating to the business cycle and recessions. I specifically enjoy the recession-based research; if we are in one, out of one, how to foresee a coming recession, how to determine which stocks will go up or down during a recession. Let me save you countless hours of time and sum it up.

Far too often you will hear a comment or read a research report to this effect: "There has never been a time that the stock market was not six months higher after the recession low was reached." How useless is this data? You will not know recession lows for months after they are hit. Another good one is when deciding what sectors to invest in: "Health care is, by far, the very best sector to invest in during a recession." Yet in the mid-2008

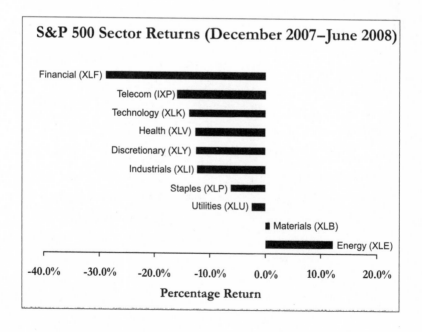

**S&P 500 Sector Returns (December 2007–June 2008)**

recession, health care as a sector has been dreadful. As you can see, it has performed as poorly as discretionary stocks!

Now, herein lies the essence of Pounce. The chart below clearly illustrates that for the first half of 2008 Materials and Energy were the best performing sectors. Remember oil at $150—a clear bubble if there ever was one? Steel stocks and farm equipment were to keep rising forever due to uncompromising global growth. Not exactly. For the last remaining six months of 2008, these sectors turned into very poor performers. This is why I truly believe buy and hold for your entire portfolio does not make sense. And I believe that an investment system like Pounce that regularly reviews and rotates your portfolio makes sense!

So, the lesson: You will do well by following the trend. Forget searching for absolutes. To say "health care always outperforms as a

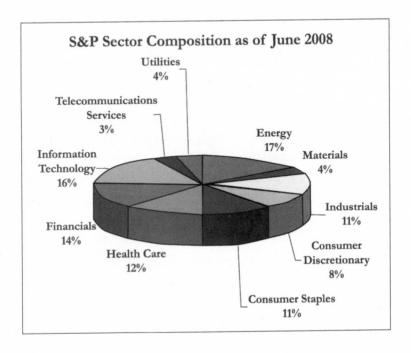

defensive sector in a slowing economy" would not have helped you during the economic slowdown that began in late 2007—at least not yet.

## THE ECONOMIC CYCLE

The economic cycle is as wonderful as it is consistent. There is very little doubt that the economy will always cycle. It would be virtually impossible to imagine a world that does not experience the four phases of the economy. This cycle has repeated not for a decade or even a century but for centuries.

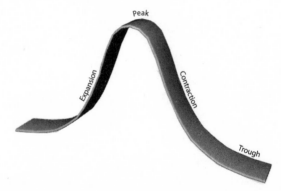

Economies move in a trend. Think of the economic cycle as a four-part process, as suggested above. This simple graph illustrates the economy. The economy expands, peaks, contracts, and forms a trough (base). Each phase is different during each cycle. The durations change, the levels of expansion and contraction change.

The Pounce investor will look for the commonalities in key indicators to determine what phase of the economic cycle we are in. This knowledge will help us pounce into and out of the right markets, sectors, and investments.

I look at these indicators to find the trend. To me, it is not so much about the specific indicators as it is about the trend and the collective effect. I'm sure one of you learned readers will tell me why unemployment can remain high and not trigger a recession, or that, if you view the yield curve using the ten-year Treasury, an inversion has only signaled a pending recession after staying inverted for at least six months. Perhaps ISM Manufacturing's numbers will not matter because we are less dependent on manufacturing. The 2001 recession still showed positive real estate trends. Yawn. You are trying to be a straight-A student and will accomplish little for your effort. I repeat, the black box that you seek is the trend—your trusting of the trend and the collective soul of the trend.

Before I show you a sample list of indicators, understand that I focused on identifying the recession. Since my firm belief is that the most important strategy is to learn to pounce down and profit or get out of the way during a recession, the first objective is to identify the coming recession. In this regard, I am far less concerned with a textbook definition of a recession. What matters is if earnings and sales for companies will slow. The second objective is to identify when the recession or the height of the slowdown has occurred (and to determine this more quickly than formal economists' reports) so we can look to pounce back up again.

How long is a trend? A one-month drop in employment or factory utilization does not make a trend. Perhaps two to three months would—so don't be so worried about being first to the party. If a new expansion or recession is upon us, it will be here long enough for you to pounce, without the risk of being the first to dip your toe in the water. This is one of the unavoidable instances where you will have to use a bit of your intuition and get a sense of what is up or down, as the case may be.

## P3 ECONOMIC SCORING TABLE

Don't let this P3 economic cheat sheet scare you. It is actually very simple. All you need to do is track six variables, and below the chart I'll explain each one. These variables are based on Leading, Lagging, and Coincidence indicators. During your monthly Personal Pounce Platform meeting, you will determine if the economy is trending higher or lower.

### P3 ECONOMIC SCORING CHART

| Consumer Confidence | Score |
|---|---|
| 3-Month Moving Average is between 90 and 100 | 1 |
| 3-Month Moving Average is above 100 | 0 |
| 6-Month Moving Average is above 100 | −1 |
| Consumer Confidence Falling 3-Month Moving Average is below 90 | −1 |
| Decreasing 3- and 6-Month Moving Averages | −1 |
| Low Consumer Confidence but 3- and 6-Month Moving Averages are increasing | 1 |
| **Consumer Credit (Ratio of Total Consumer Installment Debt and Annualized Amount of Personal Income that Month)** | **Score** |
| Ratio > 20% | −1 |
| Ratio < 20% | 1 |
| **Yield Curve Spread and Recession Probability** | **Score** |
| Probability < 25% | 1 |
| 25% < Probability ≦ 40% | 0 |
| Probability > 40% | −1 |

## P3 ECONOMIC SCORING CHART (*continued*)

| ISM Index | Score |
|---|---|
| Index Value > 50 | 1 |
| 43 < Index Value < 50 | 0 |
| 3-Month Moving Average Index Value ≦ 43 | −1 |

| Weekly Unemployment Claims | Score |
|---|---|
| 4-Week Moving Average < 375K for 4 Weeks | 1 |
| 375K ≦ 4-Week Moving Average < 400K for 4 Weeks | 0 |
| 4-Week Moving Average > 400K for 4 Weeks | −1 |

| GDP | Score |
|---|---|
| GDP within 3%–3.5% for last two quarters | 1 |
| GDP within 2.5%–3% for last two quarters | 0 |
| GDP ≧ 3.5 for last two quarters | −1 |
| GDP ≦ 2.5% for last two quarters | −1 |

**Scoring Key**
Maximum Points = 7
Minimum Points = −5
−9 = Bearish
−2 = Bearish to neutral or neutral to bearish, depending on trend; review
    last month's number for confirmation of trend
0 = Neutral
5 = Extremely bullish

**Range**

Maximum Points:    7
Minimum Points:    −9

| Bull | | Neutral | | Bear |
|---|---|---|---|---|
| −9 | −3 | 0 | 3 | 7 |

## Leading Indicators

*Consumer Confidence and Sentiment*
The consumer drives the economy, so I like viewing economic data as it relates to the consumer. The rub is, by the time an economic slowdown hits the consumer, the slowdown, or possibly a recession, is already well under way. So track the consumer for signs of an economic low, not to portend a slowdown. When the consumer indicator is used as a lagging indicator and meaningful (2–3 percent movement downward) slowdowns, defaults, and unemployment have occurred, but is not trending further lower, this could mean that a bounce back in the economy is closer than not.

Although people talk about the health of the economy based on big businesses, what really matters is the consumer, accounting for the bulk of the gross domestic product. So goes the consumer, so goes the economy.

When confidence is rising at a steady, orderly pace, one might say we are in an expansion mode of the economy. When it gaps up higher and higher to record highs—and higher—I would suggest this lends itself to an economic peak. When it gaps lower, there is a contraction in the economy and quite possibly a recession.

*Consumer Credits*
Rising debt is typical during prosperous times. Higher spikes again argue that the economy is close to peaking and could be a prelude to a recession. Once debt levels are high and defaults and bankruptcies have spiked to higher levels, I would suggest, at this point the data to be somewhat lagging and a positive indicator of the bottom.

*Yield Curve*

Based on the ten recessions since 1945, the S&P is true to form: It acts as a leading indicator selling off in anticipation of the recession; continues to decline over the next five to six months; and then recovers in anticipation of the recession's end. In all ten cases, the market's recession low turned out to be at or close to a bear market bottom. It may not be the start of a prolonged bull market. It is an incredible opportunity to pounce, with the S&P up by a mean of 16 percent three-months later and over 30 percent a year later.

What you are looking for in a positive economic cycle is a moderate rising slope with the short Treasury yield no more than 2.5 percent above three-month Treasury yields.

The predictability of the yield curve in determining a recession is often measured based on the Probit Model, with supporting work through the Helsinki Center of Economic Research. What is

### Yield Curve Spread

| Recession Probability (Percent) | Value of Spread (Percentage Points) |
|:---:|:---:|
| 5 | 1.21 |
| 10 | 0.76 |
| 15 | 0.46 |
| 20 | 0.22 |
| 25 | 0.02 |
| 30 | − 0.17 |
| 40 | − 0.50 |
| 50 | −0.82 |
| 60 | −1.13 |
| 70 | −1.46 |
| 80 | −1.85 |
| 90 | −2.40 |

A great place for yield curve data is http://finance.yahoo.com/bonds.

performed is a probability test using the yield curve spread, estimating four quarters ahead. The yield curve spread is defined as the spread between the interest rates on the ten-year Treasury note and the three-month Treasury bill. Remember, this is a model based on past data. Meaning, like all of the data and ideas suggested herein, this data should not be interpreted as a hard and fast rule. It is a guide, and to be used only as one of many tools.

### ISM Purchasing Managers Index

This survey measures manufacturing and production. Traditionally, a reading at or below 50 is negative and points to a contraction in the economy.

An interesting statistic is that, since 1950, when the six-month growth rate in payrolls has fallen below 0.5 percent, the average level of the ISM index has dropped to 46.4 percent. This creates an interesting correlation to payroll and ISM Purchasing Manager Index.

You can also use, from ISM, the non-Manufacturing Business Activity Index to get a strong reading on the direction of the economy.

### Jobless Claims/Nonfarm Payrolls

Growth in payroll is the key to spotting a peak. Several reports regarding unemployment, new claims for unemployment benefits, and jobless numbers exist. Everybody has a different tweak; it all will show the same trend. Look for initial applications for unemployment insurance as one idea. The monthly survey performed by the Bureau of Labor Statistics (www.bls.gov) tracks the percentage of employable people actively seeking work out of the total number of employable people. A 4–6 percent unemployment rate is considered "healthy." If you get too low, the government worries about inflation. Too-high unemployment and you begin to worry about a decrease in spending (recession). Or, if you have high unemployment and high energy and raw materials, it may lead to inflation.

The data supplied by the Department of Labor each Thursday is helpful (www.dol.gov/opa/medai/press/eta/main.htm). On a week-to-week basis the numbers can be volatile. Some would argue that they do not properly reflect early retirement, seasonal work, or deceased workers. Regardless, the report tracks the number of people receiving state benefits. It offers a reasonable mechanism to track if more people are filing jobless claims. As opposed to analyzing the data weekly, consider creating a four-week moving average to understand the trend.

*Gross Domestic Product*

The GDP measures output for a given country's economy. GDP is defined as the total market value of all final goods and services produced within the country in a given period of time.

$$\text{GDP} = \text{consumption} + \text{gross investment} + \\ \text{government spending} + (\text{exports} - \text{imports})$$

You can easily find this information by logging on to the Bureau of Economic Analysis.

When considering GDP, note that this information does not lead the economy; it is more of a lagging indicator. If you are tracking GDP on a monthly basis and it continues to gap higher, start looking for signs of excess and a peak—gaps higher would be a negative contrarian indicator. Five percent or so is considered above average, so use 5 percent as your base number. If you see GDP maintaining a flat number, worry about how other factors will affect stocks, valuation (earnings growth), inflation, yield curve, and sentiment.

If you see GDP recording large reductions, look at this as a bearish sign until it is close to or in negative territory. Do not try to call a bottom. The risk is too great. Once you see it leveling off at low, or even negative numbers, and valuation and sentiment also look favorable, look for some well-placed pounces.

Another problem with GDP is that it is reported usually four times for one period: First there is an advance report; then a preliminary; then a final; finally, a revised final.

## Retail Sales (A Bit of Caution)

Note that retail sales are not in your cheat sheet. Retail sales are viewed in many ways. Although many economists like to look at the sales without autos, I like to look at retail sales both, with and without autos. The trend is usually the same.

## THE RECESSION

So long as people irrationally rationalize and move in herds, so long as there is predator instinct, there will be cycles. Cycles are wonderful—especially during the recessions and the peaks. I know this sounds harsh, but why? The textbook definition of a recession is two-quarters of negative GDP. However the National Bureau of Economic Research(NBER) defines that a recession is a "significant decline in economic activity spread across the economy, lasting more than a few months, normally visible in real GDP; real income, employment, industrial production, and wholesale and retail sales." I prefer the second definition. Many instances occur where GDP does not go negative, but it declines so violently that the perception and net effect is virtually the same as a recession.

Recessions occur because of excess. While much has to do with the corporate marketplace, the GDP is predominately based on consumer behavior. It is the consumer who spends too much money as a percentage of income, often times pushing prices higher and causing inflation. The consumer, as well as corporations, leverage excessively. To curb an overheated economy and inflation, the Federal Reserve will raise short-term interest rates, which acts to slow borrowing and causes corporate profits to contract as borrowing costs are increased (this is felt the strongest with small companies, which could be attributed to the fact that small stocks sell off usually more than the large companies before the economic bottom). The result is a slowdown in consumption, which leads to a slowdown in earnings and layoffs. This causes business closings, bankruptcies, weaker discretionary spending, and so on. Often stocks will drop, and it is the consumer who stops buying, which causes a recession—which is okay if you are ready, since a recession usually causes prices to drop, mitigating inflation; stocks often sell off more than the reduction in the earnings caused, and the cycle repeats.

### Stock Market Returns During and After Recessions

| Recessions | Number of Months | During Recession | 1-year | 3-year | 10-year |
|---|---|---|---|---|---|
| Jul 1953–May 1954 | 10 | 17.94% | 25% | 100% | 179% |
| Aug 1957–Apr 1958 | 8 | −3.94% | 6% | 26% | 107% |
| Apr 1960–Feb 1961 | 10 | 16.68% | 20% | 28% | 50% |
| Dec 1969–Nov 1970 | 12 | −5.28% | 0% | 28% | 17% |
| Nov 1973–Mar 1975 | 16 | −13.13% | −27% | 6% | 73% |
| Jan 1980–Jul 1980 | 6 | 6.58% | 13% | 27% | 188% |
| Jul 1981–Nov 1982 | 16 | 5.81% | −18% | 15% | 196% |
| Jul 1990–Mar 1991 | 8 | 5.35% | 9% | 26% | 302% |
| Mar 2001–Nov 2001 | 8 | −1.80% | −1% | −3% | |
| **Average** | **10** | **3.14%** | **2.95%** | **28.20%** | **139.16%** |

I want to reiterate that recessions do not necessarily create a bear market. In fact, often bear markets aid in causing a recession. And it is important to remember that often the stock market performs well during a recession.

To review, recessions

1. Bring price stability—if there is or was inflation
2. Bring interest rates down
3. Often brings stock prices down

If the stock market drops due to a recession, it will be a longer, more violent drop than without the recession. This will ultimately lead to a stronger bull market.

The irony is that many people think a recession would also mean a lower valuation in the stock market. This is not necessarily true. Recessions usually cause lower earnings, which means lower stock prices. But sometimes earnings of corporations drop at a faster rate than the price of the stock. Should this occur, valuations as measured by price to earnings, would actually look high.

However! However! (I say the word twice, as I'm excited—and for emphasis.) Over time, the good that comes from a recession truly outweighs the bad. It gets rid of fat in the way of excess and higher interest rates and inflation—which paves the way for higher profits.

Remember, every recession has a different cause. Every recovery occurs under different circumstances. But recessions always occur, and so do recoveries. So it does not matter if the recession occurred this time under a period of low inflation versus periods of high inflation, or vice versa. Possibly the biggest argument is that typically the investor is never *sure* if we are in a recession until the economy is CLEARLY in a recession. By that time, it is often too late to make money on the downturn of the market. As a general rule, the stock market is a leading indicator, falling prior to a recession and moving higher beginning in the trough of the economy before the recovery.

## RECESSIONS AND BEAR MARKETS

We must remember that recessions are not bear markets. However, research suggests that every time the economy has gone into a recession since 1950, stocks have also been adversely affected in the short term.

Research suggests that bear markets accompanied by or caused by a recession are longer in duration and steeper in decline than stand-alone bear markets. We need to study the economy because your strategy will alter slightly if we are in or going into a bear market because of a recession as opposed to a bear market not associated with a recession.

### The Dreaded "I" Word—Inflation

Inflation is often said to be the single biggest danger to the economy and the stock market. I wholeheartedly agree on the economy, but I'm not sure I agree that it kills the market. I would suggest that the *effect of inflation* is what potentially harms the economy and the stock market. For example, think of the dramatic fall of the dollar. The dollar has literally fallen off a cliff. Yet during its worst performance, starting in 2002, the market enjoyed a great rally. An interesting aside is to consider that possibly the weak dollar may have contributed to the energy bubble, which has most assuredly contributed to inflation.

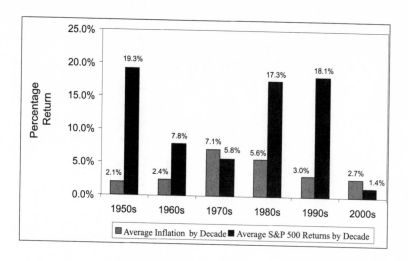

The decade leading up to the 1929 market crash enjoyed low inflation. So, the markets can rally during low inflation. However, for whatever reason, a recession was created (perhaps led in part by speculation in the stock market). The 1940s enjoyed a fairly strong market, and higher than average inflation. So did the 1980s.

In fact, a study by two Harvard economists, John Campbell and Tuomo Vuolteenaho, measured the correlation to the stock market and inflation and interest rates. Their study, covering more than seventy-five years, found that generally earnings and inflation tended to move up and down together. Stocks, as I have said, tend to move up or down based on *future expected earnings* and actual earnings trends (along with the valuation thereof).

The conclusion is that stocks are a wise investment over the long term, due to inflation.

The point is, if there is a correlation it may be a positive one for the long term. (You will need to call upon the two other Power Indicators—Investment Psyche and Valuation—in order

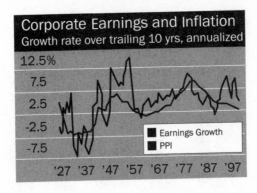

Corporate Earnings and Inflation
Growth rate over trailing 10 yrs, annualized

to make a meaningful deduction.) So, if the market drops due to perceived inflation and higher interest rates, it may be a pouncing opportunity.

| Years | Return | Inflation | Price to Earnings |
|---|---|---|---|
| 1940–1949 | 9.6% | 7.2% | 11.2 |
| 1950–1959 | 20.9% | 2.4% | 12.0 |
| 1960–1969 | 8.6% | 2.5% | 17.8 |
| 1970–1979 | 7.52% | 9.2% | 12.3 |
| 1980–1989 | 17.9% | 5.9% | 12.2 |
| 1990–1999 | 18.8% | 3.1% | 21.9 |
| 2000–present | 2.8% | 2.9% | 25.0 |

*Market Perfomance During Recessions*

An economist and investor I respect and read, John P. Hussman, Ph.D., president of the Hussman Investment Trust, studied the correlation between recessions and bear markets. His study reveals sixteen declines of at least 15 percent in the S&P since 1950 (that number has increased since the study). Of those, nine have coincided with recessions.

Considering the illustrations, it is very clear that bear markets associated with recessions were longer and more severe.

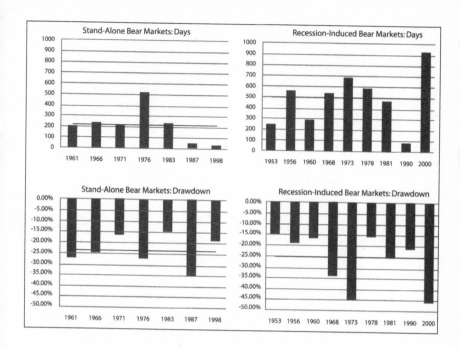

The Pounce investor, although he craves simplicity, is no fool! What Dr. Hussman's research suggests is that bear markets that are recession-induced are bad. What does the Pounce investor know above anything else? Don't lose money! In this regard, should the P3 indicators turn bearish, what do we do? Stay the course and wait it out? No, we reconfigure the Pounce Platform with investments that may possibly *benefit* from a down cycle. If a hurricane is coming, change course!

### Pouncing on the Recession

If you have clearly identified that the economy is deep in a recession, you know this will ultimately be a good time to pounce.

Major lows in the stock market have occurred during recessions. On average, the low comes five to six months into a recession.

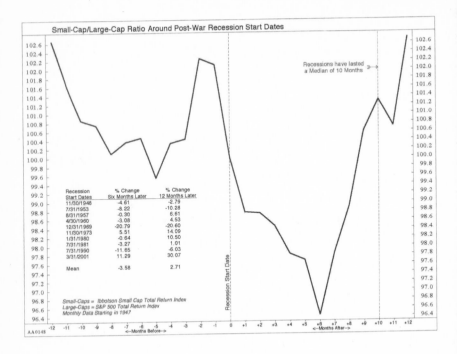

Small-Cap/Large-Cap Ratio Around Post-War Recession Start Dates

Recessions have lasted a Median of 10 Months

| Recession Start Dates | % Change Six Months Later | % Change 12 Months Later |
|---|---|---|
| 11/30/1948 | -4.61 | -2.79 |
| 7/31/1953 | -8.22 | -10.28 |
| 8/31/1957 | -0.30 | 6.61 |
| 4/30/1960 | -3.08 | 4.53 |
| 12/31/1969 | -20.79 | -20.60 |
| 11/30/1973 | 5.51 | 14.09 |
| 1/31/1980 | -0.64 | 10.50 |
| 7/31/1981 | -3.27 | 1.01 |
| 7/31/1990 | -11.65 | -6.03 |
| 3/31/2001 | 11.29 | 30.07 |
| Mean | -3.58 | 2.71 |

Small-Caps = Ibbotson Small Cap Total Return Index
Large-Caps = S&P 500 Total Return Index
Monthly Data Starting in 1947

Recession Start Date

<--Months Before-->    <--Months After-->

AA0148

This is useful information. First, it shows that based on the ten recessions since 1945, the S&P anticipates the recession by selling off into it. In all cases the market's recession low turned out to be, as NDR describes it, the bottom of a bear market. And following these lows the performance has been exceptional, with the S&P up by a mean of 16 percent three months later, 35 percent six months later, and 32 percent a year later. Obviously the trick is to call the recession bottom. Which leads to my second point . . . it's okay to be wrong about the recession bottom! In fact, the investment strategies you will use in your Personal Pounce Platform will probably not find as many stocks to buy at the height of the recession. That's all right, and it's actually safe to wait until a trend is solidified and strongly in place. Missing the very beginning of the bull market is safer, and because the Pounce Platform protects you from losing as much money during the recession, you will still be way ahead.

When the P3 economic cheat sheet shows the negative trend for the economy, it will likely mean the economy is contracting. Wait a few months and see if the trend drops lower or stays neutral. If the trend turns from negative to neutral, chances are we are working through the recession. The economy is not good, but it is not going lower. If valuation shows a bullish trend, you can invest accordingly. If valuation still shows bearish or overvalued trends, you can invest accordingly. You see, either way you get to pounce.

*When to Start Pouncing*

1. The mood has to be bleak.
2. Strong volume/big down days usually occur—capitulation.
3. Low volume, trendless days occur after the capitulation (as opposed to big spikes back up on bargain hunting).
4. Majority of your Pounce Power Economic indicators must be at low levels but cease from further dramatic gap down. So recession territory/undervalue.
5. Valuation can be higher than the long-term trend, but only if the economic cycle has bottomed and is beginning to trend higher.
6. Investor Psyche/Market Behavior must not be trending lower (unless extreme negative showing capitulation and a reversal).
7. Low earnings expectations and projections.

## EXPANSION MODE—THE FAT CAT LOSES A LIFE

The economic expansion is a glorious period filled with growth and prosperity. Most investors consider themselves geniuses during these periods, as it is hard to find major asset classes that are down. This is actually when the herd is forming, and it is the beginning of the bubbles. If one investment sector or industry is perceived to be "stronger," it may attract new money at a faster rate, causing quicker and larger price movement. Not wanting to be left behind, other investors will jump on the bandwagon, forcing the sector into extreme growth.

Ironically, the beginning of the economic expansion is not trusted. Most consumers had been bruised and battered during the last recession, and are probably thinking less about investments than they are about getting back on their feet. As I said previously, I love investing very early in the economic expansion. Although the Investor Psyche/Market Behavior is usually weak, Valuation and the Economy (two out of three Power Indicators) are positive. I consider this a very good entry point.

But as the economy gathers steam, so too will earnings and investment opportunities. This economic expansion is *usually* a great time to invest. Although the economy may expand, people might be worried about inflation or reduced profits or higher interest rates. But this has no effect on your Personal Pounce Platform. All you care about is whether valuation begins at acceptable levels, and Investor Psyche is favorable, and the economy is trending higher.

Sooner or later the good times will cease. This probably occurs right about the time you think, "Maybe it *is* different this time," and you begin to justify why the good times will last forever.

Think of the 1990s. It was a perfect investment climate: Companies were spending money on innovation; technology was increasing a corporation's profitability; consumers were spending money—and they were savvy, which kept inflation in check; earnings grew; and unemployment remained low. It was perfect. In fact, I recall reading many papers stating that, due to this new age of prosperity and technology, perhaps the economy could grow without a recession. No, it can't and it didn't. Soon stocks became too expensive. And, for whatever reason, a recession came . . . and then another after that. By the time you are reading this, an expansion has likely just begun.

This is a very dangerous time to be an investor.

I ask again that you keep this simple. Simply refer to the P3 indicators. If the economy is gapping higher and is already at extremely high readings, use the indicator to know this is a possibly a peak. If valuation is aggressive, these two indicators form a negative and cause for a more cautious stance within your Personal Pounce Platform. During your next monthly meeting, sell what the indicators tell you to sell. If Investment Psyche/Market Behavior is also showing "aggressive" signs or possibly beginning to show a negative trend, invest accordingly.

If Valuation shows any bearish trend and is confirmed by one other P3 indicator (Economic or Investment Psyche), invest your Personal Pounce Platform in "neutral" mode. If all three indicators show aggressive or negative trend, invest the Pounce Platform in "bearish" mode.

*And the Bottom . . .*

If your readings show Valuation is low, but not trending lower (bearish), this is neutral. If the eonomy has stopped going down, this would be a positive time for aggressive buying. Pounce away. If Investor Psyche continues to strengthen and the economic numbers show a bottom to a slight positive uptick, the market will likely rally swiftly and fully, although most investors do not trust this rally (since we just came through a recession). I understand this may be difficult, but trust your indicators, as well as your evolving predatory skills.

## SUMMARY

The economy is a powerful tool in calling the direction of the markets. Use your cheat sheet wisely and do not ignore what it reveals to you. If the trend is positive, check it against the P3 Valuation. It is that simple.

Recessions often lead to devastating bear markets. Do not stay the course and blindly lose money. The Pounce investor alters the investment model and reinvests accordingly if both P3 Valuation and P3 Economic are negative.

# 7

# P3: Investor Psyche/ Market Behavior

## CHAPTER NOTES

1. Don't discount Investor Psyche. Even though Value and Economic Direction are important indicators, they do not move stocks higher or lower. Ultimately only people can.

2. Understanding Investor Psyche and reading Market Behavior consists of two competing themes. The first requires you to watch what investors are doing to spot a trend, the second is to realize that most investors do the wrong thing at the wrong time. You should take an opposing view.

3. The market creates three types of great pouncing parties. First—when despair rules the day. When Investor Psyche/ Market Behavior creates a "sell at any cost mood," it usually creates a terrific buying opportunity. Since the herd usually buys and sells at the wrong time, when the herd is aggressively selling it is usually a positive indicator. The second is when the Investor Psyche/Market Behavior is strong, allowing you to run alongside of the herd. The final indicator is

when the Investor Psyche/Market Behavior is so aggressive, so positive, that it is often forming a peak. It's time to take the opposite view again.

4. The risk with the first scenario is calculating how long you need to wait for the bottom to be reached after despair rules the day. The risk with the second (and third) is to know when to get off. Get off too early and you miss the upward movement. Too late, and you go over the falls.

5. Investor psychology and market action is comprised of both "consumer mood" indicators and market technical indicators.

As important as Investor Psyche/Market Behavior is, the concept can be easily learned and absorbed. We are not day trading, so you need not concern yourself with complicated day-to-day technical analysis. A few key indicators are good enough. These indicators will alert you if Investor Psyche/Market Behavior is trending negative or positive.

Have you ever been strolling in a downtown area looking for a spot to eat? One spot is empty; the other is full of happy people munching away on their meal. Which establishment do you patronize? Most people feel that if nobody is at a particular place, it can't be all that good, and they would rather go where the crowds are. However, you have no idea what the experience will be at either place. This sums up the first principal of Investor Psyche; if no one else is buying, why should you? You shouldn't. That is, until they are extremely pessimistic—and then you pounce. Why risk the empty food establishment (unless you simply beat the dinner crowd and have a coupon)?

The goal of this chapter is to provide an objective guide

to quantifying the mood of the people and market behavior. The mood affects how people invest. The action and behavior of the market determines the direction of the market. Far too often you may think you have found a bubble that will burst or a market bottom, and you are surprised to be wrong. You probably thought the bubble had burst, or was about to burst, due to economic conditions or valuation. But perhaps you were wrong because Investor Psyche/Market Behavior was still positive. To create a system to help sift through "the noise," we will explore what the consumer is feeling (investor psyche) as well as the sentiment and action of the market using technical analysis. We will do so for markets and sectors and, to a lesser degree, individual investments.

Recently I saw that Exxon was able to have the Valdez disaster punitive damages ruling overturned—saving the company billions of dollars. Did the stock spike up? No, in fact it was off fractionally on the day of the announcement. How about the day the disaster happened? The stock experienced one of its greatest losses in the history of the company. People often have an opinion about everything—what if there is terrorism, what if the CEO is convicted of embezzling money? If that happens, the stock will most likely drop—why? There is no immediate loss. The market is perfect and collectively reflects the worth of a company based on the collective soul of the market. But still, there are cracks existing, and they are to be pounced on.

If a stock is a terrific value, what good is it if nobody buys or, worse, keeps selling? If a stock is cheap but the sentiment is negative, the negative sentiment could actually make the negative perception (baseless as it may be) a reality. If the market thinks Bear Stearns or Fannie Mae is in trouble and clients stop using their services and investors sell stock of Bear Stearns or Fannie Mae, then perception is reality. This, of course, is part of the phenomenon of herd and bubble investing. Although other factors such as valuation and economies are important, if the psyche of the investor is negative, all-out bullishness is forbidden.

During a regularly scheduled investment meeting, the team was discussing a stock we owned that was up for review to sell. The analyst who originally presented the stock recommended we keep it and possibly add to the position. When questioned as to why he liked the stock, he started out by talking about the absolute value. "Since the stock had sold off, the value was even stronger than when it was purchased." But what would drive the stock higher? They announced earnings weaker than expected—one of the worst actions for stock movement. As a result, selling volume was increasing. The analyst stated that earnings were down because the company was having some customer service issues, but, he further went on to say, "I have checked out the stores, they were very helpful. I am confident their earnings will turn around."

This scene probably plays out every day in money management rooms across the country. The analyst's argument might make sense for a pure, fundamental, deep-value investor. However, I don't want my analysts to think like this. I don't want their intuition; I want to know about measurable perception. And if perception is *turning* negative, I don't want to swim upstream. I'll look to pounce down or get out and wait until a sector is so cheap that the positive possibilities clearly outwear the negative.

The flip side to this is that, when the herd balances the seesaw with extremely violent or pessimistic moves higher or lower, I will stand on the other side of the seesaw and buy when great selling is occurring, or vice versa. Why? Because when the herd goes overboard, they are wrong. The beauty is that I believe that both situations are measurable. The caveat to this is to not stick your neck in a guillotine. Don't buy in to the height of a panic. Let some other investor be first and start the trend. Then you can jump in.

I am most excited to invest at two different periods. The first is when Investment Psyche, the Economy, and Value have reached the lowest, or close to the lowest point, as I believe the return versus the risk is exceedingly high. Despair is high. People are not buying or selling much; as such, volume is low (few investors play at this point). Value measures, as we discussed in chapter 5, are either unusually low or unusually high. Expectations for companies to grow earnings and sales are very low, usually coming at an already low period for earnings and sales. Since expectations are so low, it is often easier for companies to realize or surpass their quarterly earnings and revenue numbers. It is the perfect opportunity to pounce.

The second is when the herd jumps on the investment bandwagon. Investor Psyche is high and climbing higher, and the market's action is positive. The economy is growing, and valuation would be considered, from a historical standpoint, fair or neutral—at least at the onset. Valuation quickly gets expensive as the stock prices rise faster than the earnings and sales of the respective companies. During this period, the result is a dramatic increase in market capitalization; this is true for the market, the sector, or the stock. When the herd jumps on board, companies grow. The risk is to know when to pounce off before you go over the cliff. If there is one constant and true statement, it is when the herd gets too big, the valuation too stretched—and then the markets will reverse. Not all reversals are violent up-and-down movements; the market can stay flat for many years while the corporate growth "catches up" to valuation. This, by the way, is where I see real estate over the next several years: flat, while the world absorbs and catches up.

The Pounce investor has a secret weapon to know when to "get off" and break away from the herd. Every one of the investment strategies presented to you that can be integrated into your Personal Pounce Platform is based on screening methods that you will run periodically (once per month, quarter, or year). If you run a screen and a stock that you had previously purchased is no longer on the screen, because it no longer meets the criteria you entered, you must sell it. If a stock or sector does not meet the criteria, you do not want to own it. Never do you have to think of an exit strategy again; it's built in. Since I believe the selling discipline is difficult for most people to adhere to, the Pounce system takes out this variable by telling you when to get off and when to get on.

## THE P3 INVESTOR PSYCHE/MARKET BEHAVIOR SCORING CHART

**Analyst Opinion**

| | |
|---|---|
| 60% Bullish | −1 |
| 60% Bearish | 1 |
| All else | 0 |

**Market Breadth**
% of stocks above their 200-day
Moving Average

| | |
|---|---|
| % of stocks > 75% | −1 |
| % of stocks < 25% | 1 |
| 25% ≦ % of stocks ≦ 75% | 0 |

## Relative Strength Index (RSI)

| | |
|---|---|
| Bullish Divergence | 1 |
| Bearish Divergence | −1 |
| All else | 0 |

| | |
|---|---|
| RSI Value | |
| RSI > 70% | −1 |
| RSI < 30% | +1 |
| 30% ≦ RSI ≦ 70 | 0 |

## Scoring Key
Maximum Points = 4
Minimum Points = −4

**Scoring Range**
Score ≦ −2 : Bearish
−1 ≦ Score ≦ 1 : Neutral
Score ≧ 2 : Bullish

## PREDATORY INDICATORS
## INVESTOR PSYCHE/MARKET BEHAVIOR INDICATORS

### Analyst Opinion / Investor's Intelligence Survey

You have probably heard that most investors do the wrong thing at the wrong time. So do most professionals. Keeping with our contrarian theme, the Investors Intelligence Survey is a nifty little sentiment indicator. The IIS measures the mood of more than 100 investment newsletter writers each week. What editors Michael Burke and John Gray found was when more than 60 percent are bullish, it has been a negative signal, meaning the markets often sold off or went down. Conversely, when 60 percent are bearish, it has been bullish. This work has been repeated and studied a few times. Mark Hulbert's *Hulbert Financial Digest* is a well-respected tracking service of newsletters and newsletter

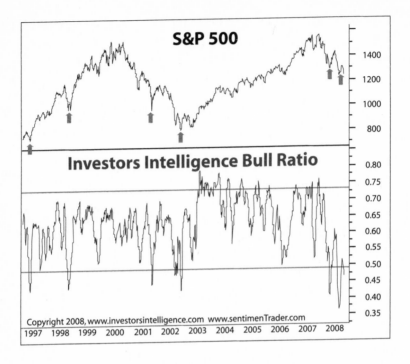

Copyright 2008, www.investorsintelligence.com  www.sentimenTrader.com

writers. His research is revealing and has uncovered many interesting facts about the success, or failure, of newsletters. Mark has
written extensively on the fact that when newsletter writers are
overly bullish or bearish the markets have more often than not
moved in the opposite fashion directive from the consensus
view.

So basically it comes back to the herd. They are usually wrong.
The more bearish a group is, the more positive the outcome, and
vice versa. In September 2007, bulls were out in force. It was not a
good sign. In March 2007 there were no bulls; the market turned
in a pretty good showing.

How accurate is this? I find it to be enormously useful. As you know, I do not use any one indicator, but this, added to all of the other tools, is very important. The bull and bear indicators usually predict three-month trends. You can get the sentiment from three different sources at: http://online.barrons.com/public/page/9_0210 -investorsentimentreadings.html.

## Market Breadth (Percentage of Stocks Above Their 200-Day Moving Average)

Often indexes are weighted based on the size (capitalization) of the company. A few stocks (the bigger companies in an index) can have an exaggerated impact on the movement of an index. What you want to know is the percentage of all the stocks in an uptrend versus the percentage in a downtrend. The answer will tell you if the market rally or sell-off is meaningful, broad-based, and has legs.

Most people just look at how an index like the Standard & Poor's 500 Index or the Dow Jones Industrial Average is doing. This is fine, but if a few companies are moving the entire index, it does not tell the whole story. During the tech bubble, a few stocks, such as Dell, Intel, Cisco, and Microsoft, controlled much of the index's movement.

By considering and charting market breadth, you will get a much bigger and better picture as to truly what is going on inside the market and within the index. The market breadth is designed to provide the investor a measure of strength or weakness in the market. It measures the number of stocks moving higher or lower.

To gauge market breadth, one of the indicators that market

technicians look at is the number of stocks trading above their 200-day moving average. This indicator is used to determine overbought and oversold levels in the market. The market is considered overbought and subject to a negative correction when more than 75 percent of stocks are trading above their 200-day moving average. In contrast, if less than 25 percent of stocks are trading above their 200-day moving average, the market is considered oversold, which means investors should expect a positive correction. This information is freely available at http://www2.barchart.com/momentum.asp and appears as below. To use this indicator, all the investor needs to do is focus on the 200-Day MA column.

**Percentage of Stocks Above Moving Average**

| Market Momentum | | Advances | Unch. | Declines | 20-Day MA | 50-Day MA | 100-Day MA | 150-Day MA | 200-Day MA |
|---|---|---|---|---|---|---|---|---|---|
| Today | +0.15% | 3035 | 220 | 2509 | 45.44% | 45.68% | 33.31% | 33.81% | 30.19% |
| Yesterday | −1.22% | 1446 | 156 | 4162 | 44.14% | 44.81% | 32.88% | 33.40% | 29.88% |
| Last Week | +0.12% | 2601 | 161 | 3002 | 60.41% | 48.11% | 36.92% | 36.62% | 32.22% |
| Last Month | +0.72% | 3365 | 124 | 2274 | 63.11% | 31.09% | 30.96% | 29.20% | 25.49% |

## Relative Strength Index (RSI)

RSI is an indicator that looks at the internal strength of a single market. RSI is plotted on a vertical scale of 0 to 100. The 70 percent and 30 percent levels are used as warning signals. An RSI above 70 percent is considered overbought and an RSI below 30 percent is considered oversold. Overbought and oversold conditions indicate that there is a good chance that the current trend will reverse.

However, for us to utilize this indicator to its fullest and take advantage of the strongest signal (divergence) that it offers, let's stop for a quick digression and talk about a tool called trendlines to identify market trend.

### Trendlines

- Uptrends consist of a series of successively higher highs and lows.
- Downtrends consist of a series of successively lower highs and lows.

Prices can only go in three directions: up, down, and sideways. A long line of past price ranges together gives you a pattern. Although there will be plenty of dips and bumps along the line, you should still be able to identify a general direction—up, down, or sideways. You can help spot this trend by drawing in trendlines.

### Drawing Trendlines in an Uptrending Market

The first thing you have to do is print, from www.chartfilter.com, a bar chart of the market index that you are analyzing.

1. Go to chartfilter.com and click on the "Charts" link at the top of the screen.
2. Type in the security or index that you are interested in.
3. Choose the "Bar Chart" option under chart style.
4. In Indicator 1's drop-down menu, choose "RSI."
5. Print the chart and find yourself a ruler.
6. When you print the chart, note the RSI value and apply it to the scoring system (RSI value) at the beginning of this chapter.

To draw a trendline in an uptrending market, connect as many successive lows as possible in a straight line. In a downtrending market, connect as many successive highs as possible in a straight line.

In a downtrending market, connect as many successive highs as possible in a straight line. Draw trendlines in a downtrending market. Downtrending lines are drawn by connecting the successive highs.

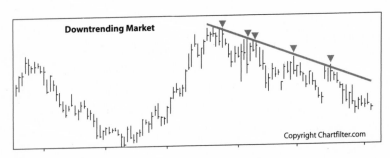

One can draw trendlines for any period of time. It can be over a day, a week, months, years, etc. We are interested in a direction that covers two to three months. Now let's combine what we have learned about trendlines with RSI.

The most important signal (although infrequent) generated by RSI is that of divergence. What we are essentially looking for is a difference in the trend between the RSI and the index. For example, if one sees that the index or a security is making new highs (positive trend) while the RSI is falling (negative trend), that is a strong signal that the current uptrend is nearing its end. This is a bearish divergence. If the stock market is reaching new lows (negative trend) but the RSI is trending higher (positive trend), that is a sign that the current downtrend is nearing its end. This is a bullish divergence.

So, how do we apply this on the chart that we just printed? Very easy. The first thing you have to decide is what your time frame is going to be. Are you going to look at a two-month, three-month, or four-month trend? Once you have picked your time frame, the first thing you want to do is draw a trendline. If the stock has been rising steadily (uptrend), then connect the successive lows from your starting-time horizon to the ending-time horizon. Then do the same thing with the RSI chart. That is, draw a trendline on the RSI chart using the same time horizon as the chart on page 144. Do you see a difference? If the RSI trendline is falling but the stock trendline is rising, that is a bearish divergence (−1). If the stock is trending lower but the RSI is trending upward, that is a bullish divergence. (+1). If both stock trend and RSI trend are in the same direction, then that is a neutral situation (0). For an example of how this should look like, see the image on page 146.

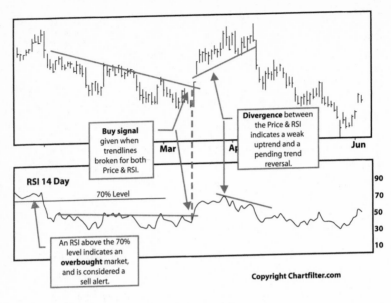

**Buy signal** given when trendlines broken for both Price & RSI.

**Divergence** between the Price & RSI indicates a weak uptrend and a pending trend reversal.

RSI 14 Day

70% Level

An RSI above the 70% level indicates an **overbought** market, and is considered a sell alert.

Mar

Ap

Jun

90
70
50
30
10

Copyright Chartfilter.com

## SUMMARY

Use Investor Psyche/Market Behavior indicator to catch the mood and future direction of the market before major reversals occur.

# 8

## Bulls, Bears, and More Foolishness
### STUDY YOUR PREY BEFORE YOU POUNCE

### CHAPTER NOTES

1. There is enough research and data on bull, bear, peaks, and stagnant markets to fill almanacs—but the knowledge is academic. You don't need to know why. You simply must know if we are in a bull market, a market that is peaking, a bear market, or a market that frequently moves higher and lower, not progressing anywhere after more than five years.

   Once you know using P3, which of these four markets we are in, you will determine how to manage your Pounce Platform and what strategy you will use to Pounce.

2. I define a bull market as a substantial increase in the price of a broad index. I define a bear market as a substantial decrease in the price of the market. A peak is a topping-out process. The Great Void is an extended period during which a market may experience cyclical bull and bear markets (short-term) but end virtually where the market

began (either including or excluding inflation). This period would be for a minimum of five years, but tends to last
longer.

3. Do not use your intuition or *think* during any one of these
   market phases. Such emotional action will cost you. It
   doesn't matter if we are in a bear market because of a housing crisis or a war. It doesn't matter if your friends tell you
   the bull in energy will never end and valuation is still cheap.
   In the short-term (periods less than two years), you don't
   need to try to determine why. You need to determine what
   market we are in, where we are going, and how to profit
   from this knowledge.

4. Regardless of the trigger, in the long term, markets will ultimately turn positive based on Valuation, Economic Direction, and Investor Psyche/Market Behavior—the three
   P3 Indicators.

5. It is your job as an investment predator to sniff early
   warning signs that the bull is ending (peak), and jump
   off.

6. Traditional secular bull markets last about fifteen years
   (mini-bear markets will occur throughout). Traditional
   secular bear markets are shorter than secular bull markets;
   however, they are usually followed by a stagnant market
   (the Great Void). Bear markets and Great Voids average
   slightly less than the average bull market. Regardless of the
   trigger, stocks will ultimately contract due to excessive valuation and a disconnect between projected and actual
   earnings. Valuation will be excessive due either to stocks
   rising faster than the corresponding earnings (actual and

projected) of the corporation or to a maturing of the earnings cycle, which can cause earnings to slow or contract, eventually causing the stocks to do the same. Although the actual trigger for when the stock will begin to decline is uncertain, valuation due to higher stock prices increasing faster than earnings (bubble effect), or unsustainable valuations due to earnings reductions, will ultimately cause market contraction.

7. The end of a bear market will provide a tremendous pouncing opportunity. It is your job as an investment predator to recognize the end of the bear and Pounce hard.

8. Having experienced one of the longest, strongest bull markets in history (one that began in 1982), many analysts feel the market is currently experiencing a Great Void. I define a Great Void as an extended period in the market during which an investor would have realized a real return of virtually zero (from point A to point B). This could be a horrible reality for many buy-and-hold investors. But for us it can be a prime pounce-on, pounce-off opportunity to "sector-rotate." During the Great Void markets will rally and contract.

9. Over ten years, stocks have outperformed bonds and Treasury bills more than 80 percent of the time. Over thirty years, they have outperformed 100 percent of the time. Stocks have never offered investors a negative real holding period return over periods of seventeen years or more.

10. The most important lesson is to not let the bear market erode the returns realized in the bull markets; and the only way to do this is to NOT BUY AND HOLD.

## BULLS, BEARS, PEAK, AND THE VOID:
## POUNCE, POUNCE, POUNCE, AND POUNCE

Many market analysts will describe the market as experiencing four phases: an expansion, a peak, a contraction, and a stagnant market.

Let's discuss the bull market, the bear market, and stagnant markets. The purpose of this chapter is to understand these phases of the market and to begin looking for patterns and cycles to help ascertain the direction of the market. Once these phases are understood, we can sharpen our predatory claws. We will then utilize the P3 to pounce and then get out of the way or ride the wave home. We will bet against the market, stay on the sidelines, or ride it up.

During every phase, the market offers the investment predator a pouncing opportunity. You must identify what phase we are in, stick to the platform you created, and try not to think too much, lest you second-guess yourself.

The first order of business is to determine the direction of the markets. This will affect your Pounce Platform, and the investment systems utilized within your platform.

### An Indicator That Works—Over the Long Term

If you are trying to determine if we are about to begin a long-term bull market, you would look at traditional valuation measurements such as price-to-earnings ratio. The Pounce investor will watch with mild interest if valuations do become historically cheap, but remember, we pounce either way. I, at least, don't feel a long-term bull is about to return any time soon.

Let's again remember why we are all here: to make great investments. As you will learn, great investments are made following the

Pounce investment strategies such as Rising Stars and Pounce for Income and Growth and placing these investments into your Personal Pounce Platform. In the short and intermediate term, valuation is not as important as knowing if the trend for the market is higher or lower. If the trend is lower, we pounce down on top of the market. If the trend is up, we ride the wave. Of all the investment strategies I present, valuation based on price-to-earnings ratio is not a major determinant for making money.

That being said, long-term bull markets lasting five to twenty years, also known as secular bull markets, will begin when the markets are undervalued as measured by valuation metrics such as price to earnings and price to sales. When these valuation measurements become cheap based on long-term averages, it is a significant sign that a secular bull is close at hand. If the stock market has historically averaged a price-to-earnings ratio of over 14 percent (hypothetically), markets would have to be significantly below this—with, say, a price-to-earnings of 12.5 percent—to be undervalued. There will likely be little interest in the beginning of a bull market, and many more stocks will appear to be undervalued than overvalued.

Secular bull markets grow and will do so for an extended period. The typical secular bull market will last anywhere from thirteen to seventeen years. One of the strongest and longest on record was the Great Bull, which started in 1982 and did not end until 2000. All bull markets will eventually come to an end. In every instance, valuation was high when the bull market ended compared to a long historical average (which would include bull and bear markets), or the average during a bull market phase. The valuation gets expensive, because eventually stocks will grow at faster rates than earnings and sales. However, if you "sold" early in the bull, when some thought the market was "expensive," you would have missed important gains and profitable investments. Meaning, as a Pounce investor, relax a bit on historical valuation measured and focus more on "what works."

What works is knowing that stocks rally for a variety of reasons. They can rally when they are considered expensive, they can rally when earnings are low. I want to repeat this: BULL MARKETS OFTEN RALLY WHEN EARNINGS ARE LOW! More important than the earnings is the analysts' estimates for earnings growth, and the company's or sector's ability to achieve this earnings estimate. You will see, when studying the tested Pounce investment strategies, that we continually monitor and favor companies that enjoy earnings upgrades as a much more important criterion than price-to-earnings ratio.

If the analysts' earnings estimates are not met, even if the growth in earnings is projected to be good, this is far more damaging than a low earnings growth year that is projected and realized.

Let me make a prediction. In October 2008 the stock market dropped in a classic emotional sell-off. The herd began to fear a recession and lower earnings expectations for companies. Once the selling began, it took on a life of its own and sold without a direct correlation to truly what a company's actual value might be. The sell-off actually added to the economic woes as businesses began to get more conservative in fear that this global recession would be as bad as some were predicting. The slowdown became a self-fulfilling prophecy. So, lower earnings will probably be realized and the sell-off was somewhat warranted. However, the sell-off went to an extreme and priced to a worst-case scenario—something that is not often realized. To this regard, if earnings in the subsequent year come in anywhere higher than the lowered expectations, I would expect a rally.

The same is true for secular bear markets. They are very long cycles. One would argue that the stock market has experienced both bull and bear markets since the market highs of 1999. While this is true, the market is trying to get back to "cheap" valuations. In this regard, one could argue that the market is experiencing one long secular bear market. Secular bear markets, including Voids, can also last for as long as a traditional secular bull market. The question is, How do you know the secular bear or the trend is over? While you don't know the specific date the market trend changes, you do know one thing for sure: Secular bull markets do not begin anew until valuation is below the long-term average (a k a cheap). So if the stock market is currently at 14.5 times earnings, and the long-term average is 13.5, one could say we are very close to starting a fresh new secular bull market. No, that is not at all what I am saying. I am saying that markets get *cheaper* than the average before they rise again.

Bear markets could happen during positive earning periods. If the rate of growth is projected higher than the earnings that are realized, stocks can begin to collapse because of uncertainty and disappointment.

How does this information help? As a Pounce investor, we enjoy tracking if we are in a bull, peak, bear, or Void. Instead of fighting the trend, we embrace it, relishing the fact that our Pounce investment strategies will work in all markets. We will slightly alter our Pounce Platform based on the knowledge of which market we are in—and, more importantly, which market is coming.

I believe that the long-term bull market is gone for a long time. I believe, based on quicker economies, faster earning cycles, and more accessible information (and people acting foolishly on this information), that bulls, bears, and Voids will happen more frequently. Further, I believe that they will happen independently of traditional valuations. During the cyclical markets that I believe we will experience for years to come, you are going to become more of a vulture, coming in and taking a few bites and then leaving. If this were a long-term bull, which it is not, you would act more like the lion—going for bigger prey and staying for a longer period to enjoy the feast. Looking for higher growth and valuation will be a secondary concern.

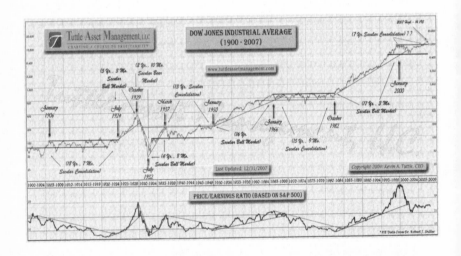

## My Two Favorite Market Cycles

As I've said, I have two favorite times to go long (betting the companies will rise) in equity investments. The first is at the bottom of the bear. This is a period when optimism has turned to despair and the demand for stocks is very light. Usually valuation is very fair. The economy could be doing well or poorly, so do not confuse a bear market with a recession. Although a bear market is experienced during most recessions, bear markets occur independently of a recession.

At the bottom of the bear, when the valuation is compelling and the expectations are low, sooner or later investors will identify this "value" and demand will begin to increase. The rising market will create further successes, creating more success. And soon a bull market rides again. One of the benefits of buying into the bear is that risk is minimized due to the potential value you receive. So in this regard, "time"—how long this value is realized—is my greatest risk, more so than market risk, since the market has already dropped.

My second favorite time to be an equity investor is during the late bull market, when silly profits are realized due to a frenzy of activity, eternal (foolish) optimism, and a powerful herd. This period is risky because, make no mistake about it, the herd will leave. No matter how great the company, sector, or market, when valuation is excessive, and optimism is great, the trend will revert. So although the profits are plentiful, serious risk abounds. It is the exit strategy that must be strictly adhered to here.

### The Great Bull Is Gone!

I read an article in a much respected magazine that stated, in effect: Don't expect another bull market any time soon. I suspect the author was referring to a secular (long bull), such as the one that began in 1982 and lasted through March 2000.

You know why this is important? First of all, 1982 was not a year in which many people owned, or had the desire to own, stocks—making it an auspicious year for a bull market to begin. Throughout the 1980s, the market climbed a Wall of Worry that included a war, a major medical epidemic, inflation, rising interest rates, another war, a junk bond bubble, the savings and loan crisis, and plenty of negative press.

The 1990s experienced a tremendous amount of negativity as well, including: a real estate boom and bust, high interest rates, fears the world would crash with Y2K, and a tech wreck on Wall Street.

But what good did it do for us to worry? Now the "experts" suggest that the profitability corporations enjoyed in the 1990s, which fueled the bull, was not the norm and would not be repeated. America will lose its edge and our corporations will lose their edge as well. Profitability in the new global economy will not be sustained and life as we know it will change. Yes, it will. Life will change. To be sure, cycles will ebb and flow. Thus, the need for pounce. So, let's go find the next bull market in the making. Or, let's go on a bear hunt and pounce on his head a while. And if we can't find a bull or bear to play with, let's find some gazelles with a broken leg for dinner.

Regardless of whether you analyze a secular bull or bear, or a cyclical bull or bear, there are stocks going up and stocks dropping, sectors going up and sectors dropping. In fact, you would prefer to invest in "stealth mode." Big bull markets attract the herd too fast. We only want the herd to rush in toward the end, moving our money to ridiculous valuations, while we make a timely exit.

## IDENTIFY THE BULL

Once we identify a bull market, your Personal Pounce Platform will seek to identify the candidates with the best exposure for growth, but, quite frankly, it's tough not to make money in a bull market. Your attention, therefore, will focus on when to get off the bull market gravy train. Although strong cyclical bull markets might enjoy gains in excess of 30 percent or 40 percent before inflation, the typical bear market sheds over 30 percent. After factoring in the time value of money and/or inflation, the net effect is usually a negligible return through the full cycle.

A traditional investment book will seek to explore how many bull markets there have been, what was the average duration, and the starting and ending P/E value. This is all interesting reading, to be sure. However, as a tool for profitable investing through any cycle shorter than a secular bull or bear market, the data is far more random. All bull markets are different. The Power 3 pouncing indicators will take what is usually incorrect, your intuition, out of the equation and allow you to use the indicators to guide you.

A bull market can be defined several ways. It could mean positive returns for market averages over a prolonged period of time. It could mean the market grows at a cumulative rate of over 20 percent for at least two quarters, or simply a market where prices rise at a faster rate than their historical average over an extended period of time. While a secular bull market is an uptrending market for an extended period of time, dissected, it really is very simple. A market that is undervalued, and unloved, begins to slowly find buyers as earnings projections are raised. Over time more buyers continue to buy into the market. Eventually valuation will move from undervalued to fair valued and ultimately overvalued as more people buy in, moving stocks higher than the corresponding earnings.

Many would argue that the market experiences frequent mini-bull and mini-bear markets comprised of 20 percent upside and downside movements. These cyclical markets are often blips in long-term trends and waves that typically last anywhere from ten to fifteen years. As an example, the bull market that began in 2004 could be considered a mini-bull market (cyclical), in a long-term (secular) bear market, or just one long Void. After many years of markets moving up and back down, at the end of the period the market is basically where it began at the beginning of the period. For the buy-and-hold investor, these periods of short-term bulls and bears are devastating! What they make in the up cycle, they almost lose entirely in the down cycle. THIS IS WHY BUY AND HOLD IS NOT A GOOD STRATEGY UNLESS WE ARE IN A LONG-TERM BULL MARKET!

## PLEASE DON'T LISTEN TO ANYTHING "THEY" SAY

- ✓ In 2000, most analysts were stating that the "correction" in technology stocks would lead to a terrific buy. Tech stocks slid another 30 percent to 50 percent.
- ✓ Very few "analysts" called the beginning of the cyclical bull market at the end of 2002. It led to one of the longest cyclical bull markets in history—more than four years!
- ✓ Many analysts said you should sell in 2005 after two years of a bull market. They stated that stocks were expensive, and that the bull would end soon. Selling in 2005 would have caused an investor to miss important gains.

Please don't concern yourself with what "they" say. Stick to your discipline: your Personal Pounce Platform. When the indicators tell you to sell, you sell. When the indicators tell you to buy, do so—and don't second guess! Do not listen to what people are saying, and do not follow your gut instinct.

Most fundamental investors will look for value (as I admittedly do) and will not overpay for stocks. I understand. Having never paid retail for my suits or my daughters' back-to-school clothes, I understand a good deal. However, if I want to make money on stocks, buying cheap stocks is not the only way to profit. We will incorporate deep value into the Personal Pounce Platform, but you will need to accept the fact that the power of the bull is so great, it will break traditional value models.

### Be Ready for the Bull to Sneak Up—It's a Tricky Beast

First, bull markets traditionally begin when investment psychology has most recently been at the lowest, or close to the lowest, point. A case in point was when the market rally began in 1982. Very few people owned stocks, and demand was quite low.

Second, a bull market rally is usually solidified or fueled by companies that are enjoying growth in their earnings. All public companies are required to report their quarterly and annual earnings. Since I often talk about earnings, let's discuss this for a moment.

As I just stated, all companies are required to report quarterly and annual earnings. Investment analysts, who might work for big companies like Goldman Sachs, or Citigroup, or for independent research firms, analyze companies and "guess" what they think a company will report for quarterly as well as annual earnings. All of these analysts' expectations are pooled, and a consensus number is published. If a company enjoys positive earnings growth, and/or exceeds analysts' expectations, this is, in my opinion, one of the most important positive actions that moves a stock higher or lower.

**It is more important that a company meet or beat earnings and sales estimates than it is to have high earnings and sales.** Wall Street hates uncertainty. A bull market can and will perform so long as companies exceed estimates. When the reverse occurs, regardless of the earnings, the bull will retreat. These numbers, as I have stated previously, are readily available on popular Web sites such as msnmoneycentral.com and yahoofinance.com.

The chart below by Ned Davis sums it up perfectly. What the line represents is the earnings growth of the companies in the Standard & Poor's 500 Index. Is it not uncanny that, soon after earnings growth went negative, a recession followed? It didn't happen every time, but often enough.

I do want to point out, however, that this is not a graph of the Standard & Poor's 500 Index, it is the collective earnings of the stocks in the index. If you consider a few of the other graphs of the Standard & Poor's 500 Index, you will see there is not a direct correlation between actual earnings and stock prices. For example,

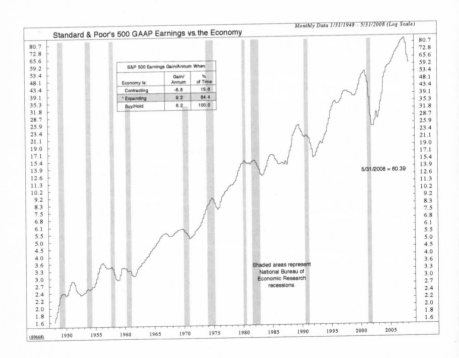

Standard & Poor's 500 GAAP Earnings vs. the Economy

Monthly Data 1/31/1948 - 5/31/2008 (Log Scale)

| S&P 500 Earnings Gain/Annum When: | Gain/Annum | % of Time |
|---|---|---|
| Economy Is: | | |
| Contracting | -8.8 | 15.6 |
| * Expanding | 9.2 | 84.4 |
| Buy/Hold | 6.2 | 100.0 |

5/31/2008 = 60.39

Shaded areas represent National Bureau of Economic Research recessions.

the great bull market that began in 1982 didn't start with great earnings. So what triggered the bull market? Ah, that is to the heart of Pounce. First, remember I didn't say that earnings had to be "great"; they simply need to be positive and exceed what analysts thought they would earn. And, in a secular bull market like the one that began in 1982, you also had low Valuation, and Investment Psyche and the Economy had reached lows. It was the perfect cocktail of all three indicators reading positive.

### Early Bull Pounce Signals

Just when you say to yourself, "No way would I buy stocks," the bull will return. Most investors miss this ideal time to invest. Yet the early alert signs that precede the bull will be evident.

1. Primarily for a secular bull market, economic indicators will often be negative or dramatically undervalued, but leveled off in terms of lack of further "gap down" indicators. This trend usually holds for at least three out of four months.

2. Investor Psyche/Market Behavior is also aggressively undervalued (panic selling). At the end of the bear, you will often see volatility increase (as expressed through the VIX Index) as more people give in to complete despair and panic selling kicks in and investors buy SPX puts (a bet that the Standard & Poor's Index will fall) regardless of how long, or the percentage drop, the market has already experienced. However, when the herd is running away from the market and your other indicators show bullish signs, be cautious and careful. Be patient and wait for the trend to bottom out. The market can remain mispriced longer than you can remain solvent.

3. If the bear market has already come and we are experiencing a trendless "Void market," consumer confidence is low but no longer dropping. Market volume is low but new lows are not increasing.

4. For a secular bull, valuation is low. To begin a secular bull market, valuation has to become dirt cheap, cheaper than the average P/E that starts a secular bull market, which is 13.5 times earnings. Markets get cheaper than the average starting point before secular bulls begin.

5. Valuation does not need to be this low for a cyclical bull market. If valuation is above the average (say 14 times current earnings), but analysts are increasing their earnings estimates above the historical average (6 percent), a bull market can begin. This actually is what happened in 2003. However, to be sure the bull is confirmed, wait until you have Investor Psyche/Market Behavior moving higher for at least one quarter.

6. Whether the bull is secular or cyclical, the constant is that analyst earnings start from a very low expectations point, and begin to ratchet higher. To a lesser extent, the same is true for sales and increases in profit margins and cash flow. Bull markets do not occur when earnings, sales, and profit margins contract. This is the one constant.

## When to Pounce on the Bull

Sometimes it will be evident to you, the self-actualized investment predator, that the bull market has seen its finest hour, a peaking process is occurring, and a contraction is imminent. Now, be careful: If you run with the bull, you might get the horns.

No one indicator will tell you when the bear will come. Nonetheless, high valuation, overheated growth economies, and highly positive investor psyche do not last forever. But don't get too excited simply because stocks become overvalued compared to their historic norms. Bull markets can and often last for a much longer period than most people expect. I was studying the most recent cyclical bull market that began back in 2003. People were saying a year into it that this bull market would not last. I retrieved articles in 2004 stating it was time to get out. And everyone had prudent reasons for this.

Even after losing 9 percent in 2000, 11.9 percent in 2001, and 22 percent in 2002, the S&P 500 Index was not cheap! Further, these experts said it would be difficult to grow earnings (despite expectations being low for earnings, which made it much easier for companies to meet them). Even though valuation was high, if you had not jumped back in, you would have missed out on several positive years.

The moral is, you are wrong and the stock market is right. As a technician would say—don't fight the tape.

So, when do you get off the crazy gravy train?

You should first consider if you should stay fully invested in the bull. Secondly, consider if you should *bet against* the bull. Betting against a market is fraught with risk. To do so without a strategy is a great way to kill great returns. My first preference is to not lose money—by taking the gains made in the bull, and waiting until the market offers another entry point in which to buy back in.

Should the indicators all point toward a window of opportunity allowing you to bet against a market (shorting a market, or buying a fund that bets against a market—a short fund), the trade must fit in with your Personal Pounce Platform. Trade only if all P3 Indicators are negative. Even if all your indicators support a trade, truly understand the transaction and the risk associated with it.

### Exit the Bull When . . .

1. Earnings expectations as measured by the consensus estimates found on most money Web sites (i.e., Yahoo! finance under Analyst Coverage) are calling for substantially higher than normal earnings growth. If the consensus of the analysts is for the market (all stocks in the index) to grow earnings in excess of 10 percent, that is red flag territory. Further, if you are seeing a slightly higher ratio of companies failing to reach these higher projected rates, as compared to the previous quarter, this is negative. It's also negative when corporations begin to modify the future earning and revenue outlook as compared to the last quarterly guidance.

2. Valuations are in excess of both the stock and the industry's historical perspective by 1.5 times. If technology stocks historically trade at 10 times earnings, and they are currently at 15 times earnings, that is a negative.

3. Investor Psyche/Market Behavior have been aggressively positive but have been slowly losing power. Although the indicators still show positive, the trend is negative. You are looking for technical patterns: new highs to new lows coming down a bit; down days on strong volume; weakening market breadth and RSI; a drop in consumer confidence over the last several months from its level six months ago. In addition, the last three months should be heading lower in each of the months.

4. Regarding Investor Psyche/Market Behavior, some analysts will look for a huge "violent" peak in the markets, evidenced

by aggressively strong readings for new highs to new lows being reached, high-volume readings, and very bullish investor sentiment readings. I do look at this data, and do believe a sell-off will occur subsequent to this blow-off top. However, after the first sell-off, investors will look at this as a buying opportunity and bid the markets back up. This is where I will start looking for the beginning of the end based on the Investor Psyche readings previously mentioned.

5. The economy can still show a neutral reading, trending higher, or even an aggressive reading. However, look for a trend comparing the economic readings to six months earlier, or a rolling average. If the numbers are so good that they are unsustainable, this will cause concern about inflation and rising interest rates, which will be, in the short term, negatively perceived.

## SUMMARY

Predators take note: bull markets will arrive, quiet as mice, with little fanfare or headlines. The mice will nibble at the cheese slowly— leaving for brief periods as they are temporarily scared away. Soon, the mice will attract the snakes, the rats, the coyotes. This, of course, attracts the really big game. Once the big game is here, this eating frenzy is almost gone; the food (liquidity) will have dried up. And, like a nomadic flock, large and small, the herd dissipates, quickly. It is very transparent, very measurable.

In the famine that replaces the frenzy (the bear market), some will lose. Others will have had the foresight to seek greener pastures (uncorrelated markets), or might just stick around to pick apart and Pounce on the defenseless prey that didn't get out in time.

Soon, it gets so bad that everyone and anyone needs to get out at any price, and they do. However, what is overlooked is the food source that has grown around them during the panic. In fact, it is time to Pounce again. And the little mice, quiet as can be, return again.

# 9

## Bubbles and Predators

### A WINNING COMBINATION

**CHAPTER NOTES**

1. Bubbles are fairly predictable, common occurrences. They usually begin to form for reasons with strong, solid underpinnings. After enough attention, they attract the masses. Fear of loss (from the investment) is replaced with greed and an unwavering belief that the bubble is justified.
2. All bubbles burst.
3. It is possible to make money while the bubble grows, but you will all too often convince yourself that it's not time to sell until it is too late, after the bubble bursts.
4. You can make money as the bubble deflates, but be careful about being too early; they tend to get bigger and stronger than anyone could possibly have predicted.
5. Bubbles occur within markets, sectors, and asset classes in general.

As you are aware, I believe most money managers fall short of delivering true greatness One of the main reasons for this is a static model. They buy the same stocks, hold on through ups and downs, and hope it all works out. Throw in diversification as an attempt to reduce risk and—voilà!—an investment platform is created. Perhaps calling it an investment platform is a bit generous.

If you possess a static model, you miss a wonderful, truly special, and potentially profitable aspect to investing—bubbles.

The purpose of this chapter is to dissect a bubble, and to discuss how they occur so that we can spot them in the making. This will provide us with the skills to decide when to participate, step aside, or pounce down on the bubble as it relates to, and fits in with, your Personal Pounce Platform.

My formal definition of a bubble is an asset class that usually begins due to sensible reasoning, excess liquidity, and an excited herd. The bubble usually bursts as the valuation is grossly overvalued and there is no more liquidity. Think about the real estate environment in 2008. It was a buyer's market. However, those who wanted to buy, and who would have qualified three years earlier, could not. Banks were hurting, due to pinched liquidity, causing stricter underwriting.

## IN THE BEGINNING

While Nikki was off occupying herself with guys who wanted to run with the bulls, Marie was working hard. You see my other sister had one goal, one focus, and that was to get a car. And she knew our old man's rule: "If you can pay for it, and keep your grades, you can have it."

Well, the big day came. She had finally saved enough and went to buy her car. Being green and environmentally friendly, she bought the brand-new hybrid that is also electric. "It's so cool," she said, "it actually plugs in—in my garage!" During that same shopping trip (these women did well!), her friend Lou bought a computer that was "strong enough" to download all her music, songs, etc. In fact, she is going to hook it up to her new plasma TV. Marie showed her car off to Nikki. Well, as you can imagine, Nikki had to have one. And if Nikki had one, everyone had to have one. A noted columnist saw this trend and wrote a story about the year's "must-haves." The must-haves included "electronics—bigger, better, and more expensive." A stock analyst created a bar graph of the increased use of electricity and electric power associated with these. He also commented that solar might be a beneficiary. A second, even more respected analyst talked about how the world was hungry for more power. He mentioned his favorite energy companies, electric utilities, energy trading companies, and a few solar companies. The stocks started to soar. One-day gains of 8 percent to 10 percent began happening more and more. A new fund was created to just track this market.

What started as a quiet growth industry turned into national attention. The skepticism about the viability and risk of the venture turned into greed, and the pride of keeping up with your neighbors and the potential humiliation of not being "in" had their place as well.

Soon thereafter, an analyst drafted a report stating that he thought things were getting a bit ahead of themselves and that perhaps the "sector was fully priced." This started a one day sell-off of 10 percent. Right after, of course, you had made an initial investment.

Well, this brought all the analysts out, stating that this was a great opportunity. Now more analysts drew more charts. The herd started buying this stuff in droves. You thought you were a genius and bought more. And then one day, it stopped.

## Great Ideas Lead to Great Bubbles

When the radio was honed into an interesting "little" device in the 1920s, it kicked off yet another wonderful craze. Since everyone had to get one, and the implications were virtually limitless; so, too, were the IPOs, new companies with new inventions promising to make people rich. It sounds eerily similar to the dot-com craze, huh? Although this invention was one of the most important inventions of the time (arguably throughout history), more people lost money on the craze than made it. In fact, of the hundreds of stocks and IPOs, only one, according to my research, remains in business today: Emerson Electric (although many might have been bought or merged).

When the automobile began to sweep the world by storm, you could imagine how many automobile and automobile-related companies rushed to sell shares in their company and watched their stocks scream higher. It was the same story, different product, same results. More people lost money as a result of speculation in the automotive stocks in the early days than made money.

The story is the same, the players are different. You have one simple job: Determine which companies are in bubble territory today, and how you will engage this beast.

## Anatomy of a Bubble

1.  A solid reason creates activity and buying interest in a specific asset class.

2. Usually credit and easy money will fuel the buying interest.
3. The herd will usually begin a frenzy of buying. Individuals try to rationalize their investments.
4. As the herd continues to jump on, one feels safety in numbers and further rationalizes that the asset prices are justified because of a far-fetched attempt at rationalizing the fundamentals.
5. This causes wanton speculation.
6. Credit tightens, valuation is questioned, and distress sets in.
7. The herd panics, poof, the bubble bursts. And then comes the panic crash.

## Why Bubbles Surprise

In hindsight it is easy to see that the technology bubble was truly a bubble. But while it was happening, it was so easy to be lured into believing it was different—this time. It was true we were quickly adopting new and exciting technology. It was true that technology would change the world. But what was not different, this time or any other, was that regardless of the promise or the lure, most bubbles start with a rational fundamental premise. But when value disconnects from an acceptable range, a bubble will form.

I began writing this book in early 2008. I wrote that by the time you will be reading this, or soon thereafter, the bubble for oil would pop. In fact, this is what I wrote in July 2008:

> "As I write, I am calling the oil and gas bubble for what I see it to be. It has not yet burst; but, alas, it will."

In October 2008, oil dropped from over $150 a barrel to under $70. The question is, Why did I feel so strongly that this was a bubble?

Like technology it was formed on a solid premise that our world needs and uses an ever-increasing amount of oil. Because only finite amounts exist, the bubble began.

The fact is, it all reverts back to valuation. I do not need to argue if alternative fuel will overtake oil, or if we have enough oil to last two hundred years, or how the green movement will change our habits. I care about the disconnect between value and the herd.

I read a report that states, "As the world grows, energy will be even more critical and this cycle of growth has just begun. Although the stocks may be a bit ahead of themselves, profits can still be made."

From the peak, oil is up more than 700 percent since late 2001, when oil was priced at $17.75/barrel. The NASDAQ only grew 640 percent through the tech bubble. Did consumption rise at the same velocity? No. In fact, worldwide consumption rose maybe 15 percent. Did production go down to restrict supply? Nope, it rose about the same as consumption. So why are oil prices so much higher? Because it is a bubble!

As you can see, consumption is moving higher at a steady, predictable pace. I could prove the point further, providing a graph of output. Output is actually moving higher, at least as fast as, if not faster than, consumption. Clearly, consumption is on the rise. But dire shortages? You have to be kidding! This looks and smells like a bubble to me!

The next time you think, "Oil, that's my thing," STOP THE INSANITY! This is how you justified the tech wreck, the real estate bubble, and everything else. If you are going to talk like that, go home, learn to become a saver (you are going to need it), invest in a staggered bond portfolio of AAA quality bonds, and never, ever try to become an equity investor.

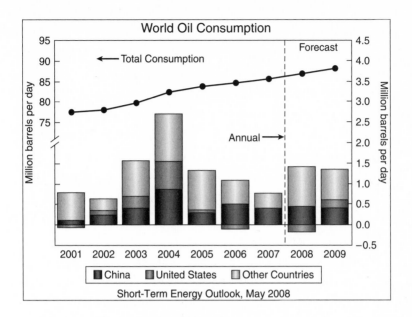

World Oil Consumption

Short-Term Energy Outlook, May 2008

### See Where Your Prey Is Going Before You Chase It: Sector Bubbles and Market Bubbles

Somewhere in the world it is 5:00 P.M., or Happy Hour. Somewhere in the world a bubble is being formed.

At one time, emerging markets such as China and India included companies that were growing at faster rates (earnings per share growth) than their stocks were growing. Could you imagine? At the time nobody cared. Investment Psyche was neutral because nobody was buying. Valuation was undervalued, and the economy was trending higher. Emerging markets were a great buy. Eventually this was recognized, the herd pounced, and the bubble was formed. Nobody believed these markets could fall. The bubble burst. Now we can look at these markets as Fallen Angel candidates (see chapter 12).

It is a mistake to focus exclusively on individual stocks, inasmuch as markets, sectors, and industries often move in a pattern.

If you take a handful of tech stocks and they are down, most likely so, too, will be the tech index. If staples are down, so, too, will the staple index be.

To the converse, rising markets tend to raise the entire index. The beauty of playing the sector, index, or industry is that you can avoid the individual stock risk, which could exacerbate the downside.

Markets, sectors, and industries tend to stay overvalued for extended periods of time, much like individual stocks. So to pounce on a bubble simply because it is overvalued is not enough. It must clearly be unsustainable and it must be dramatic. Again, some of you may be looking for a hard-and-fast rule. There is none. I use the P3 indicators. If all of the P3 indicators are pointing "aggressive," it will be cause for a pounce.

Don't pounce until you actually see fire. Consider pouncing on the bubble if the following is evident!

Although you know it is a bubble—everything points to it—you still may not pounce. Bubbles are strong and herds are hard to turn. System 2 of your Pounce Platform is designed to help you invest in leading sectors. So, in fact, you will likely be invested with the herd as the bubble is forming (however, you will be one of the self-actualized few who know how to get in and get out!).

**The Beginning of the End**
If you are investing inside of a bubble, which is likely inside of your tactical Top Gun strategy, you are instructed to rerun the screen at specific dates. If the sector you are investing in is no longer a Top Gun, the strategy forces you to sell. What usually happens if you invest alongside the herd is that strength begets strength. When the

strength starts to falter, you will be forced to sell. So, you will never be that lucky (foolish) person who enjoyed the "highest price" on your investment. It will not happen. But you will be out before the big bursting occurs. Typical for a bubble is it starts to sell off. Suckers who didn't get in early jump in. A brief rally occurs. You wonder if it was wise to sell when you did. The bubble bursts. You feel great.

You may wonder what would be a cause for a sale, and I will tell you. I remind you, however, that this is background information that helps us build our models. Inside of your investment strategies, we have already built the engine. You need to execute the strategies. The Ultra Short strategy in your Uncorrelated/Hedged portfolio might be a strategy you use when your Personal Pounce Platform turns bearish. The Top Gun strategy invests in the "top sectors" when the sector is no longer a "top" sector (as we will define); you jump ship (sell). So, you see, it is all provided for.

How one would begin to consider actually profiting from a bubble bursting (pounce down on top of the bubble) is relatively simple. If you follow the beginning to the end signals it will position you to profit from a bubble burst. Before making a move, you actually want to see the bubble start to go down:

- All P3 indicators must be showing clearly aggressive.
- You and the herd are convinced that the ridiculous expectations are justified, but they are simply unrealistic.
- Future *world-changing* projections are, however convincing, impossible.
- There are grossly exaggerated valuations—at least two times historical values. (If P/E averages 10 times earnings, 20 times

earnings would be the start—regardless of promised expo-
nential earnings growth.)

- Violent and quickly rising stock prices, 5 percent moving days not uncommon.
- A new ETF is created for this asset or sector.
- Is an obsession in the media (e.g., oil).
- You are chastised and ridiculed by all who hear you even suggest that the asset or market is a potential bubble. To prove this, call your ten smartest friends and tell them you think Chinese and Indian markets are in bubble territory and you think they are headed lower. I'll bet you dollars to donuts they will try to talk you out of it. My proof! This is the Ken Stern equivalent of what is called the Retail Investor Indicator. By the time the retail investor is investing, the bubble is almost ready to burst.
- The technical details tell the story. The RSI may still be high, but the index is steadily slipping. The index is much higher than the 200-day moving average. And many of the stocks within the sector are starting to fall. Also look at money flow. You want to see if money is flowing into or away from the stock. If money flow starts to go negative, the beginning of the end could be close.
- If there is a hint that the economy might be slowing, it could lead to lower consumption and a "miss" on the already lofty earning expectations.
- Everything reverts to the mean eventually.

Although these indicators signal the beginning of the end; don't bet based on what your gut tells you. Wait until the bubble comes to you. RSI has to start trending down, valuation has to be excessive, and the bubble drops big on a few big down days (and suckers buy back in thinking it a great deal).

## A Recent Bubble

Let's take a stroll down memory lane. Remember when the computer hardware sector started to take off in 1994? Although the stocks moved up consistently, it was not until 1997 that this sector went from Rising Star to a bubble pattern in terms of excess valuation. It is simple to see, when you look at the growth compared to earnings, just how excessively this bubble was formed.

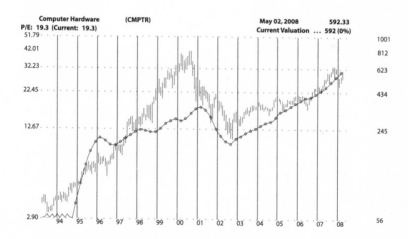

Notice how clear this bubble is when we view just one indicator: earnings growth in the preceding chart, and P/E based on the earnings chart, as illustrated on top of page 178:

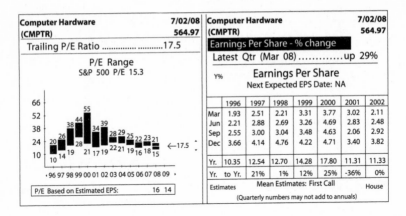

| Computer Hardware | | | | | | 7/02/08 |
| (CMPTR) | | | | | | 564.97 |

Trailing P/E Ratio ................ ...........17.5

P/E Range
S&P 500 P/E 15.3

P/E Based on Estimated EPS:          16  14

| Computer Hardware | | | | | | | 7/02/08 |
| (CMPTR) | | | | | | | 564.97 |

**Earnings Per Share - % change**
Latest Qtr (Mar 08) ............up 29%

Y%  **Earnings Per Share**
Next Expected EPS Date: NA

| | 1996 | 1997 | 1998 | 1999 | 2000 | 2001 | 2002 |
|---|---|---|---|---|---|---|---|
| Mar | 1.93 | 2.51 | 2.21 | 3.31 | 3.77 | 3.02 | 2.11 |
| Jun | 2.21 | 2.88 | 2.69 | 3.26 | 4.69 | 2.83 | 2.48 |
| Sep | 2.55 | 3.00 | 3.04 | 3.48 | 4.63 | 2.06 | 2.92 |
| Dec | 3.66 | 4.14 | 4.76 | 4.22 | 4.71 | 3.40 | 3.82 |
| Yr. | 10.35 | 12.54 | 12.70 | 14.28 | 17.80 | 11.31 | 11.33 |
| Yr. to Yr. | 21% | 1% | 12% | 25% | -36% | 0% | |

Estimates          Mean Estimates: First Call          House
(Quarterly numbers may not add to annuals)

From 1996 to 2000, P/E went from a high of 20 to a high of 55. Yet earnings growth at its best was 25. This clearly shows me that it would have been smart to start watching for weakness in this bubble in 1997, when the P/E was three times the rate of earnings growth! By 1998, the multiple was crazy and you would be taking profits regularly to keep your weighting commensurate with your original investment. By 2000, as the bubble bursts, you are "all out."

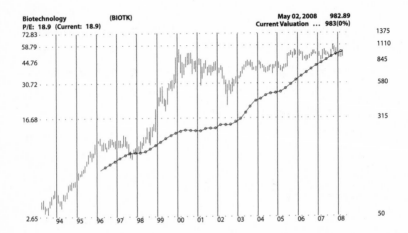

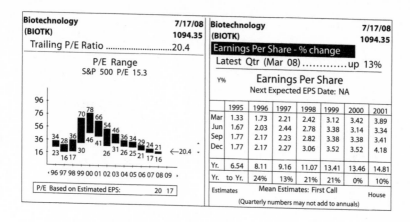

Look at biotechnology. Almost the exact same bubble pattern emerged with biotech as did with technology. The solid line represents earnings. The sector traded in line with the earnings until the middle of 1998. From there the stock soared at a faster rate than earnings. Do you find it as interesting as I do that earnings for biotech continued to climb at a rapid pace but the sector basically trended nowhere since 2003 until now? What this shows me is that this Fallen Angel (see chapter 12) would not move higher until the earnings caught back up to the stock price, creating a "fair value" situation. Wow, almost like having the answers to the test the night before!

Look at the earnings growth compared to the P/E ratios. Wow! How cool is this? In 2000, right before the bubble burst, P/E ratios were as high as 78 yet earnings growth was 0 in 2000 or possibly 10 percent in 2001. A total disconnect. Do you see? Isn't that just mind-boggling how easy it is to spot a bubble? Everyone jumped on this biotech craze, knowing it would be years and years and years before profits would come from this sector.

However, now that earnings have caught up to the stock prices, it might be time for this Fallen Angel to spread its wings once more.

## Ready to Pounce

Since we talked about energy, let's talk about a very specific sector: fertilizer.

This is a fairly new bubble being formed, but, make no mistake, it is a bubble.

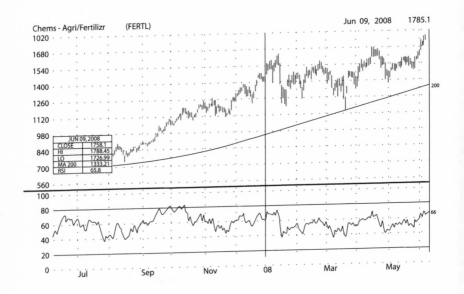

Here is a bubble that has strength and momentum. The RSI is moving into an overbought situation. The solid line represents the 200-day moving average. The stock has risen well above this average. This is a classic case of a bubble forming. But, in the words of the Ginsu knife commercial, "Wait, there's more."

Analysts are still "very excited" about the sector. In fact, the 2009 projected earnings per share are 27 percent. The P/E ratios

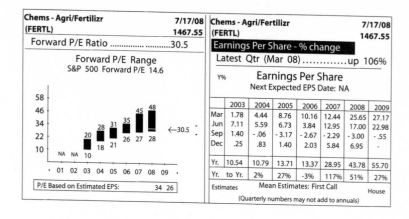

are as high as 48 times earnings. High, but perhaps not exceedingly high if the sector actually achieves the earnings growth projected for next year. This is the reality; few companies, sectors, and or markets can achieve and sustain earnings growth of 27 percent. So when the analysts come out with a report stating, "Ah, we were a bit 'aggressive' in our earnings forecasts," the earnings will be lowered, and the P/E will then be way too high and this bubble will burst.

### NEWS FLASH

The bubble burst pretty hard. Odd, isn't it. People didn't stop eating. Yet the stocks that comprised this industry fell like a rock off the Empire State Building. Maybe we should start looking at this sector as a Fallen Angel?

### Just One More Example—It's Really Good

This one has me really laughing hard. In fact, I so enjoy this sector and the stocks within it that here I illustrate a specific stock as well as the sector. Previously we have reviewed only the sectors.

Well, solar *is* the next source of fuel, isn't it? Is it un-American of me to say this is a bubble? A $280 stock trading at 33 times sales, with virtually no P/E? I don't even need to give you any more of the technical or fundamental data. Go ahead and pounce away.

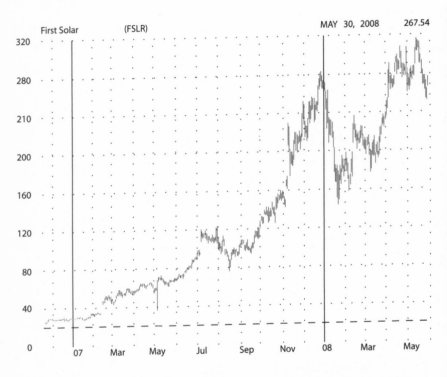

First Solar is actually cheap, right? The analysts are projecting 100 percent earnings growth, so a P/E of 148 is justified. Come on.

Let's have more fun with FSLR. It trades at 35 times sales! In Rising Stars we like to look at stocks averaging price to sales of 1.5, not 35! Look in the top left-hand portion of the screen. The market cap represents the value of the company based on total outstanding shares and current price. If you wanted to buy the company, it would

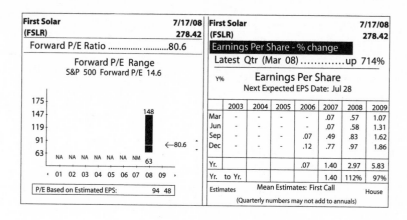

| First Solar (FSLR) | 7/17/08 278.42 |
|---|---|
| Forward P/E Ratio ...............80.6 | |

Forward P/E Range
S&P 500 Forward P/E 14.6

| | | | | | | | 148 |
|---|---|---|---|---|---|---|---|
| 175 | | | | | | | |
| 147 | | | | | | | |
| 119 | | | | | | | ←80.6 |
| 91 | | | | | | | |
| 63 | NA | NA | NA | NA | NA | NA | NM 63 |

‹ 01 02 03 04 05 06 07 08 09 ›

P/E Based on Estimated EPS:    94 48

---

| First Solar (FSLR) | 7/17/08 278.42 |
|---|---|

**Earnings Per Share - % change**

Latest Qtr (Mar 08) .............up 714%

Y%    **Earnings Per Share**
Next Expected EPS Date: Jul 28

| | 2003 | 2004 | 2005 | 2006 | 2007 | 2008 | 2009 |
|---|---|---|---|---|---|---|---|
| Mar | - | - | - | - | .07 | .57 | 1.07 |
| Jun | - | - | - | - | .07 | .58 | 1.31 |
| Sep | - | - | - | .07 | .49 | .83 | 1.62 |
| Dec | - | - | - | .12 | .77 | .97 | 1.86 |
| Yr. | | | | .07 | 1.40 | 2.97 | 5.83 |
| Yr. to Yr. | | | | | 1.40 | 112% | 97% |

Estimates    Mean Estimates: First Call    House
(Quarterly numbers may not add to annuals)

---

| First Solar (FSLR) | 7/17/08 278.42 |
|---|---|
| Market Cap ($ bil) .......................22.2 | |

Key Ratios & Measures

Price to Book ...........................19.3
Price to Cash Flow...................... 123
Price to Sales .........................35.03
Cash Flow to Earnings .....................1.2
Return on Equity (Margins) .......19.8%
Enterprise Value / EBITDA ...........115
% LT Debt to Total Capital .............. 6%

Insider Trading - Last 3 Months

---

| First Solar (FSLR) | 7/17/08 278.42 |
|---|---|

**Revenues - % change**

Latest Qtr (Mar 08) .............up 194%

Y%    **Revenues**
(in Millions)

| | 2003 | 2004 | 2005 | 2006 | 2007 | 2008 | 2009 |
|---|---|---|---|---|---|---|---|
| Mar | - | - | - | - | 67 | 197 | 379 |
| Jun | - | - | - | - | 77 | 217 | 448 |
| Sep | - | - | - | 41 | 159 | 289 | 528 |
| Dec | - | - | - | 53 | 201 | 335 | 581 |
| Yr. | | | | | 135 | 540 | 1,038 | 1,880 |
| Yr. to Yr. | | | | | 273% | 106% | 81% |

Mean Estimates: First Call
(Quarterly numbers may not add to annuals)

cost you $22 billion to buy all the shares outstanding at $278 per share. Yet it only has $1.880 billion in sales. Regardless of the growth, it is a foolishly expensive bet.

## How to Play the Bubble

Assume you are invested in the bubble as it begins to rise. The hardest part will be to know when to exit stage left! Don't use your crystal ball or your gut.

Remember, every investment strategy inside Systems 1, 2, and

3 in your Pounce Platform will use the bubble extensively to profit. You will learn to invest early in your Core System using primarily the Rising Stars strategy. You will learn how to ride the leadership inside System 2: Tactical/Top Gun. Finally, you will determine, in System 3, how to play current bubbles and bubbles that have already burst. This is where you will learn strategies such as Hedging, Pair Trades, and Ultra Shorts.

If you know something is overvalued, why would you still own it? In System 2 of your Personal Pounce Platform, you invest in "the best" sectors. It is extremely important to be invested in the leadership sectors—even ones, such as energy, that become overpriced. Without owning in these sectors, your return would be dramatically reduced. For example, if you had invested in the S&P during 2007, from January 1 through December 31, your return would have been 5.5 percent. However, if you had not owned the two best sectors, materials and energy, your return would have been 1.72 percent.

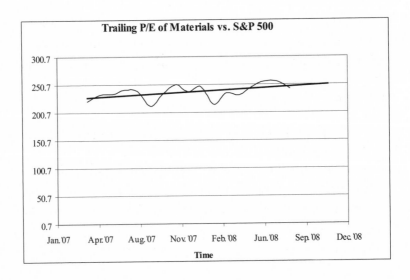

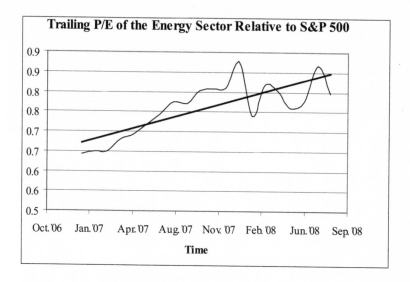

However, when the bubble begins to fizzle and Investment Psyche turns negative, you quickly exit, rather than trying to convince yourself that the sell-off is a buying opportunity. Again, the Top Gun strategy of your System 2, is your tactical trade. We buy leadership and exit when a stock no longer is a leader.

If the P3 indicators measure "aggressive," this would set up for a bearish Personal Pounce Platform. If a bearish platform exists, you will utilize investments designed to profit from those sectors in which bubbles are bursting.

## BURST BUBBLES AND PREDATORY TACTICS

If a bubble formed for a viable reason, at some point, after the bubble burst, it would be logical to assume that a burst bubble would offer a viable ratio of reward to risk. In the case of biotechnology, the stocks grew on the promise of potential earnings and sales. Now that the sales and earnings are a reality, this would be a viable investment sector to begin researching. In the case of solar, the simple fact that it falls does not justify your pouncing.

Biotech burst in 2001. This bubble did not ripen to a point that I would consider it until seven years later.

Your investment strategies will find the bubbles for you. They will probably be included in your Fallen Angels screening process. Some investors will look at the names of the sectors and stocks that will start popping up on your screen and they will say, "Oh no, I lost money when Japan dropped." Yes, they did. And that is why you are getting the bargain on Japan fifteen years later!

When investing in a burst bubble, be it simply a chart you like to watch or through a screening process, relax and take it slow. This is not a quick-trigger trade. Finesse it, do not muscle it.

You may use the following as a loose guide.

*Reenter the Broken Bubble.* This, along with virtually all the strategies presented in Pounce, should be finessed as opposed to muscled. Use your skills, tools, and strategy as opposed to your gut reaction (or action, as the case may be).

So, how do you know when to get back in? You guessed it! Begin using P3.

Valuation: The bubble will revert to fair value, or less than fair value (that is, the stock will be cheap). You may consider investing when:

1. Price to earnings is < long-term growth rate
2. Earnings per share has grown for the last two quarters faster than the benchmark (Standard & Poor's 500 Index)
3. EPS is projected to rise in the next quarter
4. Price to sales $\leq$ its 5-year average

5. Revenue is projected to grow at a faster rate next year than in the previous year

Investment Psychology/Market Behavior: Even if absolute value is recognized, don't bottom-feed. Jumping back into a burst bubble requires a bit of activity and positive market behavior.

1. Look for at least two months of positive RSI for the stock or the industry
2. Look for accumulation and/or an increase in volume

Economy: It is not as critical with this strategy. However, if the economy is in free fall, you will need valuation to be that much cheaper, and you will want absolute buying in the sector before pouncing back in. If the economy is strong, your window will be tighter. It is during this economic phase that valuation can be a bit stretched; however, you still want solid market behavior. If the burn is still fresh, and nobody buys, the investment will be dead money for quite a while.

## Playing the Bubble

Stocks can stay overvalued and in bubble territory for extended periods of time. Simply because they are overvalued does not warrant selling. Real estate was overvalued for at least a few years. As I write this, I can think of at least five situations that many traditional value managers would consider overvalued: energy, fertilizer, certain water utilities, electric utilities, and emerging markets.

Go back and look at what the experts were saying in 2004— "The stock market is overvalued." In fact, because of earnings growth, the stock market was only slightly overvalued, and not only did it not justify short positions, it still justified many long positions.

## FUTURE BUBBLES

There are bubbles forming all the time. They are actually not hiding or afraid of publicity. In fact, they thrive on the attention. Watch the news and read the paper. Ask your know-it-all neighbor where the next great investment is (a sure bubble forming, right?). When you see a subject talked about over and over, you will find a bubble. The subject could be energy, gaming, or even wind power. It could be about a meat disease, or any number of situations that cause a market class to go higher. Use the cheat sheets presented in this chapter to determine: (a) if you are invested in a bubble, and if you will be slowly stepping out of the bubble during your monthly meeting; or (b) if the bubble should be put on watch mode to pounce down on. When you hold your monthly Personal Pounce Platform meeting, you will have completed the necessary research and be ready to pounce down on the bubble if the indicators align and allow you to do so.

In addition to simply "paying attention" prior to my monthly Pounce meetings, I print out a list of stocks. You could do this in almost any stock screening program, from Yahoo! to Zacks.

In the screen on page 189 I kept it very simple, as that is how I feel all investment strategies should be. Let people complicate them. I searched only five variables, which yielded eight names. I searched 2008 price to earnings that were at 30 or greater and prices to sales of 10 or greater, with a current price of 10. Finally, I did add that the earnings were expected to increase by at least 10 percent in the next year. I did this to weed out any potential Fallen Angels. I like what I found: many financial companies, some material companies, and a few other added names. First Solar, no surprise, was on the list. Two gold names as well. Bingo. As I write, my P3 Economic Indicators show the economy close to a bottom, stocks at slightly less than fair value, and Investment Psychology at extreme negative (which is a positive). If the markets begin to rise, so, too, should the dollar, and this could have a negative impact on gold. This simple screen was a useful guide to future bubbles.

From here, we can decide if the stocks themselves deserve to be watched to short, or determine what sector the stocks are in and begin to watch to pounce on it, the latter being the preferred, more conservative strategy. If any one specific industry or sector dominates screens like this, it is a fair assumption that this sector is probably in extreme bubble territory.

| Company Name | Ticker Symbol | P/E 2008 | P/S 2008 | Price per shr 7/21/08 | Price % chg 6 mths | Ern % chg '09 vs. '08 |
|---|---|---|---|---|---|---|
| Agnico Eagle Mines | AEM | 75.5 | 17.87 | 71.52 | 0.3010 | 0.65 |
| Celgene | CELG | 47.7 | 14.17 | 71.51 | 0.3060 | 0.55 |
| Capitol Federal Fin'l | CFFN | 61.0 | 18.21 | 38.64 | 0.3500 | 0.28 |
| New Oriental Edu ADR | EDU | 59.1 | 14.02 | 74.50 | 0.2630 | 0.38 |
| First Solar | FSLR | 95.4 | 21.61 | 281.18 | 0.5990 | 0.98 |
| Goldcorp | GG | 45.8 | 11.98 | 46.12 | 0.3380 | 0.22 |
| Randgold RSC ADR | GOLD | 45.2 | 10.74 | 51.59 | 0.2270 | 0.24 |
| Rex Energy | REXX | 141.7 | 10.02 | 21.68 | 1.0510 | 0.41 |
| Royal Gold | RGLD | 43.4 | 18.38 | 37.55 | 0.2060 | 0.31 |
| Research In Motion | RIMM | 51.4 | 10.80 | 115.03 | 0.2990 | 0.69 |

## NEWS FLASH

The previous chart is nothing short of stunning. Gold tends to do well during slow economies. When I first ran this on July 21, 2008, the economy was clearly slowing and gold was continuing in popularity. But this is a perfect case of a solid reason for a bubble, but a disconnect to value. Subsequent to July 21, many stocks dropped in value as the bear market raged on. But the fact that this screen produced stocks that dropped more than the market, and with many gold stocks, is truly a testament to the Pounce philosophy.

## SUMMARY

There is a valid economic reason for most bubbles attracting the crowd. Bubbles grow beyond any and all justification. The crowd always finds a reason to justify the bubble. Bubbles burst, always and every time.

To not invest with the leadership while the bubble grows will dramatically limit your return. Not buying "deep value" is not a reason to feel guilty. You are not stealing from the cookie jar, nor do you need to go to Confession.

What you must not do is become greedy. You must not veer from your sell discipline. Take the bubble for what it is—a pouncing opportunity. Enjoy the ride and get off when the investment strategy dictates.

## BOOK THREE

# POUNCE

## The Personal Pounce Platform

**IN JUST A FEW CHAPTERS,** you've learned what most analysts on Wall Street never figure out. The main impediment for most individual investors is gut instinct overriding prudent investment decisions. To combat this, we will now create a structured investment process that relies on sound, tested investment strategies, screening for those stocks predisposed to win regardless if we are buying or selling. This process culminates with the Personal Pounce Platform.

As we have learned, the Personal Pounce Platform consists of three systems. System 1 is Core. System 2 is Tactical. System 3 is Uncorrelated or Hedge.

The specifics of your Personal Pounce Platform will depend on whether the P3 indicators tell you the market is bullish, bearish, or neutral. Most of the same investment strategies are utilized for each market. However, if the market is bullish, you will have more stocks that make the cut (I refer to the screening process that filters out the select stocks). Further, the Personal Pounce Platform allows you to allocate a higher percentage of your assets to each investment. When markets reach a peak or turn bearish, not as many stocks will make the cut. If you do not have as many stocks to invest in, by default what will remain is a higher cash position. Further, as our P3 indicators turn bearish, the Personal Pounce Platform reduces the percentage of funds you can allocate to any one stock.

I will list every possible investment strategy that may be included in your Personal Pounce Platform.

# Core: Rising Stars and Pounce for Income and Growth

## CHAPTER NOTES

1. Rising Stars and Pounce for Income and Growth (PIG) are my two favorite strategies to use within System 1: Core of your Personal Pounce Platform. We will deploy both strategies inside of your Core Personal Pounce Platform.

2. When the P3 indicators are trending higher, winning stocks are Rising Stars, characterized first and foremost by their earnings growth and ability to exceed the analysts' expectations and, second, by the multiple that is paid for the company. The trick is to be fully cognizant of the fact that earnings growth will slow, and that a key component of this strategy is to jump off. If you fail to jump—you will get pounced.

3. Pounce for Income and Growth is an important core strategy, as it tackles an entirely different component. Dividends have always been an integral part of an investor's total return. This is perhaps less so in great bull markets (like the one that ended in 2000), but dividends are now once again a factor.

Searching for both income and growth will be a secret weapon in your strategy.

4. Shooting Stars are stocks that are not fundamentally sound and do not possess the quality of the fundamentals or the technical strength to support their often higher price. Rising Stars often become Shooting Stars once the irrational herd jumps aboard. A predator must avoid Shooting Stars. Although they are hypnotic, they are simply too quick and too risky to participate in. Remember, everything will eventually revert to the mean.

The purpose of this chapter is to create a methodology to discover both Rising Stars and PIG, as well as to separate the companies that truly fit these strategies from the impostors that could cost you money. Once the discovery is made, you will then determine how and when to utilize these strategies within your Personal Pounce Platform (PPP).

## RISING STARS

Rising Stars/Growth and Reasonable Prices (GARP) is one of my primary investing strategies. Don't misunderstand me, I use more than one trading platform, just as I wear more than one color suit. But on average, this is my comfort zone. I believe companies that increase their earnings faster than their peer group and faster than the market as a whole are worthy of consideration. If they are reasonably priced, I believe this offers the sweet spot for risk versus reward.

A Rising Star is an individual security, industry, sector, or market that has the potential to appreciate at a faster rate than that of the overall market. If a Rising Star is growing at an expected rate in relation to the sector and the market, then we focus on this first. We focus on the price that is paid for this growth second (price to earnings and price to sales).

Rising Stars can be purchased in any economy, but we are most cautious if P3 indicators are negative and the Personal Pounce Platform is bearish or neutral. During these environments you will see that the Rising Star screen will produce fewer stocks. When your Personal Pounce Platform is bullish, the Rising Star strategy will produce more stocks.

## Shared Traits: Less Guts, More Glory

It is human nature, but people always gravitate to names. I fly American Airlines, so I should check out their stock. I enjoy drinking Starbucks coffee, so perhaps I should buy shares. I shop at Home Depot, and it is busy, so I will look to invest.

Sometimes this is a sensible idea, and sometimes these stars will make the list. However, often the big glory stocks have big overhead (it costs money to keep the big boxes humming) and are very cyclical.

Think outside the box, if you will. Perhaps more glory comes from the companies that support the big names. What computer systems do they use? Who are their suppliers? Where are the employees buying their uniforms? Who owns the real estate of the big box?

To truly be a Rising Star, the company should be of quality. I like solid profit margins. They don't need to grow exponentially every year, but the company should be profitable enough to withstand the impact from any downturns by maneuvering or lowering prices. A Rising Star should have a solid business model and preferably be part of a macroeconomic trend. During bear and Void markets, dividend stars are more important. During all periods, rising cash flow is a sound quality in a Rising Star. Of course, sales and earnings growth continue to be met with positive guidance from the company. If the company fails to deliver positive guidance, chances are you will have a Fallen Angel on your hands.

## RISING STARS REVEALED—THE CHEAT SHEET

As a professional money manager, I have access to certain analytical tools that perhaps you may not. And while I may prefer some of my indicators, you can create a perfectly useful Rising Star screen right on moneycentral.msn.com or finance.yahoo.com or www.zacks.com. If you have never created a screen before, don't fear. It is step by step, and, as with everything I do, it is simple!

To create the Rising Star screen I am going to give you two choices. Choice one, go to my Web site, kenstern.com. Click on "Alpha" and click on "Rising Star Screen." You can simply download or print the results.

Or you may wish to do it yourself. Perhaps you will download the data as an Excel spreadsheet. Or keep certain records. Or, from time to time, change the parameters as you get adept at creating screens. Should this be the case, repeat the steps I laid out in chapter 2.

## RISING STAR SCREEN

1. Price $\geq$ 10
2. Market cap $\geq$ $1 billion
3. 5-year historic earnigns growth $\geq$ 1.20 percent of the industry median (meaning 20 percent higher than the industry)
4. 5-year historical sales growth $\geq$ 1.20 percent of the industry median (meaning 20 percent higher than the industry)

5. Positive change in next year's earnings per share (EPS) estimate
6. Price-to-earnings growth ratio < 1.6
7. Price to sales ≤ 1.5
8. Debt/total capital ≤ 50 percent

This beautiful, simple, powerful screen is more valuable than you can even begin to realize. Used in conjunction with your other investment strategies and incorporated into your Personal Pounce Platform, it is the Holy Grail. Don't simply consider this "interesting"; implement it.

## Rising Star Implemented

1. On the day of your Personal Pounce Platform meeting, run the screen.
2. Resolve to and subsequently sell any stocks from the previous month that do not fit the screen.
3. The one exception: If you are within a two-month holding period to qualify for long-term capital gains tax treatment, wait for two months before selling the stock.
4. Consider those stocks that the screen reveals as Rising Stars. You will find fewer stocks in bearish or neutral (Great Void) market periods, probably averaging less then five. You will find a larger number of stocks in bullish periods (more than ten).
5. If your Personal Pounce Platform is bullish, you will allocate 50 percent of your System 1 to Rising Stars. To implement this, buy the same percentage of each stock to total 50 percent. However, in a bullish Personal Pounce Platform, no

one stock can equal more than 5 percent of the total amount of money allocated to System 1—meaning that, if so few stocks are produced by the Rising Star screen, you will not be fully allocating the 50 percent. As an example, if three Rising Star candidates are produced, and the Personal Pounce Platform is bullish, you will allocate 15 percent—5 percent to each stock in this strategy.

6. If your Personal Pounce Platform is bearish, allocate 30 percent of System 1 to this strategy. The same 5 percent max per security rule applies.

7. If neutral, the maximum amount allocated to this strategy is 40 percent, and the same 5 percent rule applies.

One point of clarification, which will be further discussed in chapter 13. You'll review your Personal Pounce Platform monthly, but once you've decided on a direction—bullish, bearish, or neutral—you shouldn't change it or the strategy for a period of three months. So, conceptually, you may have a bullish Pounce Platform that you are hoping to change to bearish because your P3 indicators now show bearish. Don't change unless or until you've been bullish for at least three months.

### Does Rising Stars Work?

This system has amazed me. We back-tested it from January 2000 through June 2008, figuring the period included both cyclical bull and bear markets. The total return on this hypothetical back-test exceeded 266 percent. By comparison, the Standard & Poor's 500 Index was flat for the same period.

The turnover (the number of stocks bought and sold within a year) was high, averaging about 63 percent per month. Because of this, and the relatively low number of holdings, this strategy would not be suitable for everyone. The trading costs, added to the limited number of holdings, would cause an unfavorable risk/reward ratio. Remember that back-tests can be different and provide different results than real-time actual investments. This is not meant to provide you with a conclusion to simply go out and implement this strategy. Like all strategies, it contains risk and you can lose principal.

As a rule of thumb, I would argue that you shouldn't put less than $50,000 in Rising Stars as outlined. A viable alternative would be to run the same screens and see if a trend develops with most of the stocks in a similar industry or sector. Should this be true, you may be able to invest in that industry using an Exchange Traded Fund.

## RISING STAR CASE STUDY

Let's review industries and companies that may be considered Rising Stars, and the thought process behind each. A big macro theme right now is infrastructure: building globally and growing globally, as well as repairing and fixing old buildings, roads, and bridges here in the United States.

During these discussions, everyone loves talking about the China funds, the glitzy real estate companies and the snazzy companies that will occupy these buildings. But what about investing in a company that is behind the scenes but crucial? Consider Manitowoc (MTW),* a builder of giant industrial cranes. These screens were created by typing in "MTW."

---

* At the time of this writing, Ken Stern and/or Ken Stern & Associates owned shares of Manitowoc and may own shares at the time you read this.

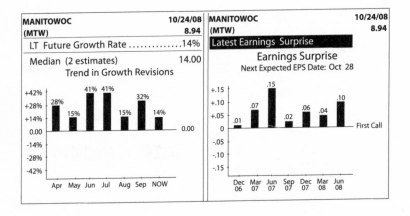

I am very pleased at MTW's ability to continue to surprise to the upside on their earnings. Yet the stock has continued to drop. The sell-off is probably due to fears that the worldwide need for their product will slow due to slowing industrial growth. Even if this is true, remember that absolute value is what is important. If a qual-

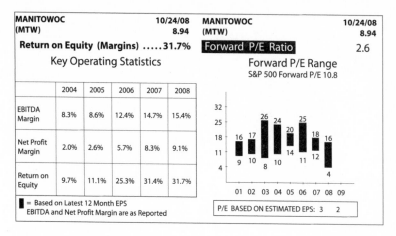

| | 2004 | 2005 | 2006 | 2007 | 2008 |
|---|---|---|---|---|---|
| EBITDA Margin | 8.3% | 8.6% | 12.4% | 14.7% | 15.4% |
| Net Profit Margin | 2.0% | 2.6% | 5.7% | 8.3% | 9.1% |
| Return on Equity | 9.7% | 11.1% | 25.3% | 31.4% | 31.7% |

ity stock with strong sales and earnings can be had on sale, it might make a sensible Rising Star.

Throughout the global expansion the margins and Return on Equity rose significantly. Lower stock price and higher earnings have driven Price to Earning ratios down. Obviously now the thought is, earnings will go down causing Price to Earnings ratios to go higher. However, earnings would have to drop dramatically for a number of years to justify this low valuation.

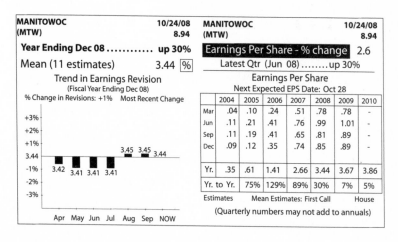

| | 2004 | 2005 | 2006 | 2007 | 2008 | 2009 | 2010 |
|---|---|---|---|---|---|---|---|
| Mar | .04 | .10 | .24 | .51 | .78 | .78 | - |
| Jun | .11 | .21 | .41 | .76 | .99 | 1.01 | - |
| Sep | .11 | .19 | .41 | .65 | .81 | .89 | - |
| Dec | .09 | .12 | .35 | .74 | .85 | .89 | - |
| Yr. | .35 | .61 | 1.41 | 2.66 | 3.44 | 3.67 | 3.86 |
| Yr. to Yr. | | 75% | 129% | 89% | 30% | 7% | 5% |

| MANITOWOC (MTW) | | | | 10/24/08 8.94 | |
| --- | --- | --- | --- | --- | --- |
| Revenues - % change | | | | | |
| Latest Qtr (Jun 08) ........up 28% | | | | | |

Revenues
(in millions)

| | 2005 | 2006 | 2007 | 2008 | 2009 | 2010 |
| --- | --- | --- | --- | --- | --- | --- |
| Mar | 510 | 633 | 862 | 1,077 | 1,333 | - |
| Jun | 590 | 746 | 1,019 | 1,305 | 1,514 | - |
| Sep | 565 | 779 | 1,006 | 1,261 | 1,452 | - |
| Dec | 590 | 775 | 1,118 | 1,358 | 1,485 | - |
| Yr. | 2,254 | 2,933 | 4,005 | 4,984 | 5,452 | 5,865 |
| Yr. to Yr. | | 30% | 37% | 24% | 9% | 8% |

Mean Estimates: First Call
(Quarterly numbers may not add to annuals)

| MANITOWOC (MTW) | 10/24/08 8.94 |
| --- | --- |
| Revenues - % change | |
| Latest Qtr (Jun 08) ................ .up 28% | |
| Latest 12 Months ...................up 31% | |

Market Cap ($ bil) .......... .............1.2

Key Ratios & Measures
Price to Book .................... ...........7
Price to Cash Flow ......................2.3
Price to Sales ............................26
Cash Flow to Earnings ..................1.2
Return on Equity (Margins) .... ...31.7%
Enterprise Value / EBITDA .........31.7%

As you can see, earnings have come down, as would be expected in a global recession. However, does the new earnings numbers justify the stock price?

With healthy revenues, low Price to Cash Flow and low Price to Sales, the value proposition looks very compelling. Another criteria that a bit further research would offer is the amount of debt. If they do not have cash to weather the storm and had high amounts of debt, a further red flag would be raised. MTW currently has less then 11 percent debt.

### CASE STUDY—TEVA*

Don't you just love looking at a chart where a stock is dropping yet earnings and relative strength is increasing? I do.

How many other businesses support a margin of over 20 percent with a decelerating Price to Earnings Ratio? In fact, very few.

---

* At the time of this writing, Ken Stern and/or Ken Stern & Associates owned shares of TEVA and may own shares at the time you read this.

TEVA PHARM ADR          (TEVA)
P/E: 14.8  (Current: 14.8)
3.79

Oct. 24, 2008  38.7
Current Valuation ... 39(1%)
56

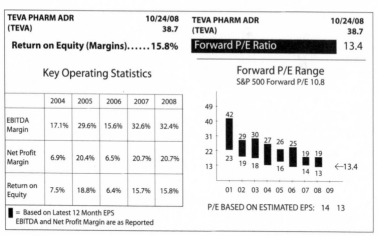

| TEVA PHARM ADR | 10/24/08 |
|---|---|
| (TEVA) | 38.7 |

**Return on Equity (Margins)......15.8%**

### Key Operating Statistics

|  | 2004 | 2005 | 2006 | 2007 | 2008 |
|---|---|---|---|---|---|
| EBITDA Margin | 17.1% | 29.6% | 15.6% | 32.6% | 32.4% |
| Net Profit Margin | 6.9% | 20.4% | 6.5% | 20.7% | 20.7% |
| Return on Equity | 7.5% | 18.8% | 6.4% | 15.7% | 15.8% |

■ = Based on Latest 12 Month EPS
EBITDA and Net Profit Margin are as Reported

| TEVA PHARM ADR | 10/24/08 |
|---|---|
| (TEVA) | 38.7 |

**Forward P/E Ratio**              **13.4**

### Forward P/E Range
S&P 500 Forward P/E 10.8

Bars: 01 42/23  02 29/19  03 30/18  04 27/16  05 26  06 25  07 19/14  08 19/13  ←13.4

P/E BASED ON ESTIMATED EPS:   14   13

Revenue has been increasing faster than the market, yet the multiples of Price to Cash Flow and Price to Sales are actually lower than the industry. The price to sales appears a bit high at 3.05 times sales and I suppose it is on the surface. However, when you compare it to the industry, it is actually on the very low end.

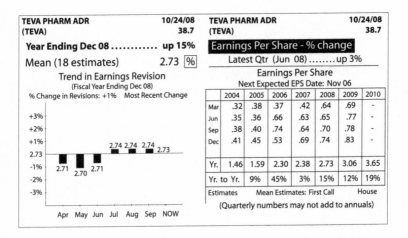

| TEVA PHARM ADR (TEVA) | | | | | | 10/24/08 38.7 |
|---|---|---|---|---|---|---|

**Revenues - % change**
Latest Qtr (Jun 08) ........up 18%

Revenues
(in millions)

| | 2005 | 2006 | 2007 | 2008 | 2009 | 2010 |
|---|---|---|---|---|---|---|
| Mar | 1,305 | 1,673 | 2,080 | 2,572 | 2,925 | - |
| Jun | 1,227 | 2,172 | 2,386 | 2,823 | 3,208 | - |
| Sep | 1,317 | 2,286 | 2,366 | 2,894 | 3,168 | - |
| Dec | 1,401 | 2,277 | 2,576 | 2,998 | 3,313 | - |
| Yr. | 5,250 | 8,408 | 9,408 | 11,297 | 12,472 | 13,729 |
| Yr. to Yr. | | 60% | 12% | 20% | 10% | 10% |

Mean Estimates: First Call
(Quarterly numbers may not add to annuals)

| TEVA PHARM ADR (TEVA) | 10/24/08 38.7 |
|---|---|

**Revenues - % change**
Latest Qtr (Jun 08) ............... .up 18%
Latest 12 Months ...................up 14%

Market Cap ($ bil) .......... ............31.6

Key Ratios & Measures
Price to Book ................... ...........2.1
Price to Cash Flow .....................12.0
Price to Sales ...........................3.05
Cash Flow to Earnings .................1.2
Return on Equity (Margins) ..... .. .15.8%
Enterprise Value / EBITDA .......... ...9.9

| TEVA PHARM ADR (TEVA) | 10/24/08 38.7 |
|---|---|

**Year Ending Dec 08 ............ up 15%**

Mean (18 estimates)      2.73  %

Trend in Earnings Revision
(Fiscal Year Ending Dec 08)
% Change in Revisions: +1%   Most Recent Change

| | | | 2.74 | 2.74 | 2.74 | 2.73 |
| 2.71 | 2.70 | 2.71 | | | | |

Apr May Jun Jul Aug Sep NOW

| TEVA PHARM ADR (TEVA) | | | | | | | 10/24/08 38.7 |
|---|---|---|---|---|---|---|---|

**Earnings Per Share - % change**
Latest Qtr (Jun 08) ........up 3%

Earnings Per Share
Next Expected EPS Date: Nov 06

| | 2004 | 2005 | 2006 | 2007 | 2008 | 2009 | 2010 |
|---|---|---|---|---|---|---|---|
| Mar | .32 | .38 | .37 | .42 | .64 | .69 | - |
| Jun | .35 | .36 | .66 | .63 | .65 | .77 | - |
| Sep | .38 | .40 | .74 | .64 | .70 | .78 | - |
| Dec | .41 | .45 | .53 | .69 | .74 | .83 | - |
| Yr. | 1.46 | 1.59 | 2.30 | 2.38 | 2.73 | 3.06 | 3.65 |
| Yr. to Yr. | | 9% | 45% | 3% | 15% | 12% | 19% |

Estimates     Mean Estimates: First Call     House
(Quarterly numbers may not add to annuals)

Most recently analysts have actually revised earnings higher. Although the most recent change is only a 1 percent increase, in a deep recession, an increase of any kind is a big positive in my book. Further the earnings per share is actually expected to drop a bit in 2009 but rise again in 2009. I view this as a very healthy trend.

## WHEN TO STEP OFF A RISING STAR/ SELL DISCIPLINE

For me, the sell discipline is simple and mandatory. During your monthly Personal Pounce Platform meeting, you will run the Rising Star screen. If you are doing it manually, you will have to simply run through the checklist. If a stock that you own does not make the list for the new month, it is to be sold. It does not matter if you think it is a good stock, if you are down, if you want to just "wait and see." You sell.

### One Exception to the Sell Discipline

Should the Rising Star strategy be used in a non-tax-qualified account, and you are within two months of a long-term capital gain on the stock, consider if it is warranted to hold the stock for at least twelve months to qualify for long-term capital gains treatment.

### Caveat, Disclaimer, Word of Caution

This strategy will incur many short-term gains and losses. This may adversely affect your taxes. Get professional tax advice. Also, make sure you have a low trading cost platform.

## SHOOTING STARS

Some stocks that look like Rising Stars are actually shooting stars. They look great but burn out fast. Shooting Stars can be found in the same place that bubbles can be found. Please review the screening process for bubbles (chapter 9). A few examples include:

✓ New high lists combined with . . .

✓ High-volume leaders, combined with . . .

✓ Price-to-sales ratio over 4, combined with . . .

✓ Price to earnings double the long-term growth rate

✓ Your neighbor claims to be getting rich off one of these stocks or sectors

✓ A new ETF is being formed for the industry or sector

## POUNCE FOR INCOME AND GROWTH MODEL:
## THE LAZY PREDATOR'S SALVATION

This is a wonderful strategy for System 1: Core of your Personal Pounce Platform. It is to be used with Rising Stars. In fact, it is another excellent way to skin the cat. These are stocks with high income, but which do not move in direct correlation with the parameters we demand in Rising Stars.

Similar to Rising Stars, during all three Personal Pounce Platforms, bullish, bearish, or neutral, you will seek out and screen for Pounce for Income and Growth. Similar to Rising Stars, you will sell when a stock no longer makes the grade. You will sell regardless of whether you like the company or have made or lost money. Unlike Rising Stars, you DO NOT screen monthly. You will only screen for Pounce for Income and Growth once per quarter.

Dividends have historically been an extremely important component of the "total return" on an investment. Investors seem to have all but stopped caring about dividends midway through the 1900s. Searching for companies with superior dividends and the ability to consistently increase them was a very large component of most investors' models, and for good reason.

Alas, during long-term bull markets, especially the most recent in memory (1982–2000), investors focused on growth and searched for companies with superior potential for capital appreciation. Income was virtually off the radar in the selection process. Income was considered stodgy, boring, or "old-fashioned."

Well, many smart old-fashioned folks can run longer marathons and pounce for many more decades thanks, in part to the income from worthy corporations. An income stock will rarely be at the top of the list in terms of performance or appreciation (that's okay, you have enough at the top, and the top will eventually end lower). Income should allow you to pounce without getting you out of breath.

From 1959 until 2006, compounded dividends have accounted for 76 percent of the S&P total return.

According to IDC via FactSet Research, if you took the "bear market" as expressed from March 23, 2000, to March 31, 2003, the non-dividend-paying stocks realized a negative return of 25.23 percent, whereas the dividend-paying stocks were up 9.63 percent.

## Screening for PIG

When looking for dividend-paying stocks with growth potential, search and Pounce on those companies that have a strong history of paying and increasing dividends. You're searching for those companies that are committed to continue to both pay and increase their dividends. Many of these companies (sometimes referred to as dividend aristocrats) are committed to their dividend policy and will work hard to continue it.

## PIG SCREEN

1. Dividend yield $\geq 3\%$
2. Market value $\geq \$1$ billion
3. Next 3- to 5-year EPS growth $\geq 7\%$
4. % change in price $> -20\%$ (meaning the stock cannot have fallen more then 20% over the last three months)
5. Return on equity (ROE) 5-year average $\geq 10\%$
6. % change in current quarter estimates (last four weeks) $> 0$

### PIG Implemented

1. Every three months, on the day of your Personal Pounce Platform meeting, run the Pounce for Income screen.
2. Resolve to and subsequently sell any stocks from the previous quarter that do not fit the screen.
3. The one exception is that if you are within a three-month holding period to qualify for long-term capital gains tax treatment, wait for two months before selling the stock.
4. Consider those stocks that the screen reveals as PIG. You will find fewer stocks in bearish or neutral market periods, probably averaging less than 5. You will find a larger number of stocks in bullish periods (more than 10).
5. If your Personal Pounce Platform is bullish, you will allocate 50 percent of your System 1 to Pounce for Income. To implement this, buy the same percentage of each stock (equal weight) to total 50 percent. However, in a bullish Personal Pounce Platform, no one stock can equal more than 5 percent of the total amount of money allocated to System 1. If so few stocks are produced by the Pounce for Income screen,

you will not be fully allocating the 50 percent. As an example, if three Pounce for Income candidates are produced, and the Personal Pounce Platform is bullish, you will allocate 15 percent—5 percent to each stock in this strategy.

6. If your Personal Pounce Platform is bearish, allocate 30 percent of System 1 to this strategy. The same 5 percent max per security rule applies.

7. If neutral, the maximum amount allocated to this strategy is 40 percent; the same 5 percent rule applies.

### Does the PIG Strategy Work?

You would likely be surprised to learn that PIG has performed as well as it has. Due to some of the strict parameters inside of this screen, you should note that the strategy is not necessarily less volatile than Rising Stars. It simply tackles the Core of your portfolio from a slightly different angle.

Using the same period beginning in 2000 and ending in July of 2008, the average total return was over 150 percent. The turnover is high, averaging over 65 percent, however; remember it is a screen that is run every twelve weeks, not every month. Like any back-test, actual results can vary. Past performance is no guarantee of future results. You can lose principal.

As you read the screens you should be excited, squirming, itching to go. These simple screens may very well be your gateway to Pouncing Power.

### SUMMARY

You now have two complete systems to use. You will take the findings these systems provide and implement them within your

System 1: Core of the Personal Pounce Platform. Trust in the strategy. You will find that simply having a strategy already gives you an edge. And the fact that the strategy is a solid strategy gives you more than an edge. It gives you Pouncing Power.

# 11

# Tactical Investing: Top Gun

## CHAPTER NOTES

1. Tactical investments are investments designed to take advantage of an existing situation. They are, by nature, designed to be purchased for a specific reason, and sold when the reason no longer justifies the investments.

2. For your Personal Pounce Platform, you are going to execute the investment strategy we refer to as Top Gun. Top Gun investments can be made by purchasing Exchange Traded Funds or Mutual Funds or Stocks.

3. The Top Gun philosophy embraces leaders in earnings or the top performers in an asset class. You will create either three of four asset classes from which to choose a leader. This section of your Personal Pounce Platform will have either three or four investments (comprised of ETFs) and/or cash depending on whether your Personal Pounce Platform is bearish, bullish, or neutral.

4. Don't feel guilty that you are buying a leader. You, unlike the rest of the herd, will jump off before the mean reverts. At some point, asset classes that are the leaders will not be the leaders. We recognize this and plan for it through the Top Gun model.

If you want stocks that will make money and beat the market, buy top performers. For the purposes of this model, we define a top performer as the best-performing asset class in a certain predetermined group, and/or the sector that enjoyed the highest upward revisions to earnings estimates. No other valuation screens were used.

You may be biting your nails right now. I know, the first time I tried it I felt like it was cheating. Most investors invest based solely on traditional valuation methods. When you deviate from this, it feels a little awkward. I'm telling you—I'm with you! It took many personal evaluations and counseling sessions and much soul searching to come to grips with reality. The reality is: Just because I strongly believed something for so long does not make it correct. And what I believed was that if I bought cheap stocks, they would eventually grow. Wrong. The same realization swept over me when I realized that buying and holding stocks or funds or any asset class forever was not the best way to the promised land.

Let me show you the system. Then you can decide if it is right for you.

## SYSTEM 2: TACTICAL LEADERS/TOP GUN

Creating the Tactical Leaders platform will be simple and almost completely objective. Once established, it requires minimal thinking and work. The ultimate goal is absolute global return. We'll seek a positive net return regardless of the benchmark return used in System 1. The system will identify investments in the top-performing sector or asset class, in three different investment universes.

You will reevaluate the holdings every three months.

For maximum efficiency and effectiveness, I will choose widely used, unmanaged ETFs for the holdings inside of System 2. ETFs are usually liquid and trade like any other stock.

Leadership systems all have a slight variation or adjustment to make their system special. Analysts may create regressions or use complex mathematical formulas to pinpoint optimally suited times for buying and selling the leadership. They will formulate their own system to determine what they believe to be salient data; leadership based on earnings growth, asset performance, etc.

I believe, regardless of how you tweak it, that a leadership system will add value as long as you know when to get off the train. Everything reverts to the mean, eventually. It pays to be in leadership, but leadership is not constant. At some point, it will fizzle out and your job is to take your loot and run.

### First: Choose the Asset Classes

Investment Universe 1: Domestic Sectors
Investment Universe 2: Domestic Capital Value and Growth
(Large, Mid-, and Small Cap. Value and Growth)
Investment Universe 3: International Sectors

*Universe 1—Domestic Sectors*

| | |
|---|---|
| SPDR Energy | XLE |
| SPDR Discretionary | XLY |

| SPDR Staples | XLP |
| SPDR Financials | XLF |
| SPDR Health Care | XLV |
| SPDR Industrials | XLI |
| SPDR Materials | XLB |
| SPDR Technology | XLK |
| SPDR Utilities | XLU |

*Universe 2—Domestic Capital Value and Growth*

| SPDR Large Cap Growth | ELG |
| SPDR Large Cap Value | ELV |
| SPDR Mid-Cap Growth | EMG |
| SPDR Mid-Cap Value | EMV |
| SPDR Small Cap Growth | DSG |
| SPDR Small Cap Value | DSV |

*Universe 3—International Sectors*

| SPDR Emerging Markets Small Cap | EWX |
| SPDR International Mid-Cap | MDD |
| SPDR International Small Cap | GWX |
| SPDR Emerging Asia | GMF |
| SPDR Emerging Europe | GUR |
| SPDR Emerging Latin America | GML |
| SPDR World Ex-U.S. | GWL |
| SPDR International Dividend | DWX |

## Disclaimer

This is not a recommendation to invest exchange-traded funds. Please consult your investment professional and thoroughly review prospectus for risks, fees, and expenses prior to investing.

## Second: Implement

Set up three trading days. The first date will be at the beginning of every year (the actual date is less important than that the sector be held for a minimum of one year). The second date should coincide with the end of the second quarter, so trade in the beginning of July. And the third trade should coincide with the end of the second quarter or the first days of the third quarter.

In each sector you will choose the top-performing sectors, as measured by returns from the previous year (based on the last twelve months—not calendar year). Invest the same percentage in each of the three categories. The performance should be based on a rolling twelve months, from the last date of the quarter that most recently ended. Of the 100 percent that you invest in System 2, you will equally weight 33.3 percent per allocation to total 100 percent. However—and this is important—if either of the top two performers has been a top performer for over eighteen months (in which case you would be buying that holding after it has been a leader for over one and a half years), you will skip that sector in favor of the next highest performer. This is also true when you run the screen for the next quarter. If one of the sectors you hold has been a leader for over eighteen months, go to the next best performer.

## Ken, Are You Truly a Predator, or Have You Become the Prey? This System is Ludicrous!!!

The system is not ludicrous. Leadership leads. In fact, we analyze and reanalyze these types of systems often. Not only do I feel that leadership systems have the ability to outperform markets, I believe the risk as expressed through deviation and volatility is commensurate with that of a similar strategy where people rebalance into the weakest sectors.

In fact, by rotating into the leadership through size, indexes, etc., you are mirroring the mood of the Economics and Investment Psychology powers. Valuation admittedly could be stretched and skew on the high side. With a sell discipline, and refraining from buying into a third year of outperforming, risk is mitigated.

Let me once again state that I believe buying into leadership is more beneficial on a risk-adjusted basis than rotating into the losers.

## OVERACHIEVER VARIATION

### Variation 1—Top Gun Earnings Revisions

As a personal note, this is the version that resembles what we at Ken Stern & Associates use. It is obviously a bit more labor-intensive to implement but the returns reflect the work.

Again, I modified the screen so you can do this using the moneycentral.msn.com site. The trick is that you are still trying to find a leadership sector; however, you are doing it not by stock performance but by using analysts' upward revisions to earnings to find top performance. This screen is specific to the Standard & Poor's top sector.

1. Screen for all stocks that have upward revisions in the last four weeks.
2. Filter to screen for only one sector at a time.
3. Do this for all sectors. You might wish to choose not to include Telecom, as it is so small it may skew results.
4. Go to standardandpoors.com to determine how many companies there are in each sector.
5. Divide the number of revisions by the total number of companies.
6. The one with the highest number of revisions is the one you invest with.
7. Repeat once per quarter.

Many of you overachievers may wish to enhance this even further. Feel free. However, let me remind you of what I said at the beginning of this book: If you try to be a straight-A student . . . This simple screen, as basic as it may be, produced stellar results.

From the beginning of 2000 until July 2008, the back-tested return would have been in the range of 250 percent, cumulative. Since the Standard & Poor's 500 Index returned roughly flat in the same period, I would say this is not too shabby. The key to this strategy, as with many of our strategies, is remembering to run the screen every quarter and to sell the stocks that do not make the new list. This strategy using risk measurements such as beta and deviation is not less volatile (a k a less risky) than the Standard & Poor's 500 Index. That means you need to get off the ride when the screen tells you to!

However, tinker away as tinkerers do. It may occur to you that many stocks that do enjoy an upward earning revision still suffer losses. One variation of the above model might be to screen out all the stocks with negative momentum even if they enjoyed upward revisions.

The stocks with negative momentum but with analysts' upgrades should be placed in another filter, perhaps added to your Fallen Angels.

I hope you feel, as I do, that this is like a meat processing plant: Everything gets used, from the hoof to the steak. After all, we are in the business of pouncing. And we are predators.

## Variations Continued

There are many variations that you may wish to implement and fold into the model. I like many of them, and believe they can add alpha; it is simply a matter of how much time, energy, and resources you have available.

Another variation is to add a fourth universe. Select ETFs that focus on specific global industries, such as biotechnology, real estate, water, natural resources, commodities, and gold. By investing in specific sectors and industries, the volatility increases. However, if you catch the Rising Star, enjoy the leadership, and remember to exit in a timely manner. This strategy may further your pursuit of gains. One variation would be to narrow your hold and review period to six-month intervals to verify that your holding maintains its position as a leader.

At Ken Stern & Associates, we use a similar system for tactical trades for applicable accounts. However, instead of simply choosing the top sectors, we use a complex regression that focuses on earnings and performance.

As has been proven in several models over infinite time periods, strength begets strength and leadership begets leadership. The markets are right, and for whatever reason, leading asset classes will lead for a reason. Usually, leading asset classes will lead because of the same powerful P3 factors; the value is compelling on a growth basis, the economic direction for that asset class is positive, and ultimately the Investor Psyche/Market Behavior for that asset class is positive.

The common scenario is that the asset class starts with a modest valuation but with earnings growth exceeding that of the peer group and the rest of the market. Early predators nibble on these investments until they begin to increase in price and prove their earnings and sales power. At which point, more investors move in, creating a positive demand. Soon the herd gets carried away, valuation becomes excessive, and the leadership sector goes to the back of the line. (Think birds in V formation flying south for the winter.)

## USE WITH 401(K) PLANS

If you believe that the market over the next several years will have a great deal of movement, but not really go anywhere, then the conventional buy and hold approach inside your 401(k) might not cut it. Indeed, many people have seen their 401(k) earn little since the beginning of the decade. A trendless market is a bit more palatable inside your 401(k) assuming you are adding new money every month and assuming you have a long, long time before you need the money. Many of us need a better strategy for managing our 401(k).

Pounce may be able to help. Prior to discussing Pounce specifically, you have some work to do. First, you have to make sure your 401(k) plan has great investment choices. Look for representation in many different asset classes, hopefully many of which are uncorrelated. Of course the plan should include small-, mid-, and large-cap offerings both on the growth and value side. But, you should also have many sector funds that may not be correlated. This could be domestic and international bonds and equity. It might also mean natural resources, real estate, and other specific sectors.

401(k) providers are compelled to have an investment committee that reviews, at least annually, the investment choices within the plan. Send these ideas to the committee. Consider asking to be part of the committee.

Now that this is established, what about considering using a Top Gun approach inside the 401(k)? It is hard to discuss specifics as so many plans offer so many (or few) choices. But as a general rule, break the 401(k) down by the various bond choices, international equity, and domestic equity. Invest in the one or two leaders from each of these sectors and consider reviewing the Top Gun every other month, or every quarter. For example, say you compare as one of your choices all domestic equity. Assume that the Top Gun is the small-cap value fund. Two months later you review the best performer and it is now Large Cap Growth; consider rolling into this fund.

This strategy will really have to be tweaked and modified depending on your specific 401(k). All 401(k) choices are different so it may or may not work with yours. But at least consider it.

## SUMMARY

Tactical is simple and effective. Buying the leaders is objective, and it works so long as you know when to get off. You get off when the sector is no longer a leader. Regardless of whether you are searching leaders through earnings revisions or through stock appreciation, success is successful. It is a somewhat difficult and, at times, uncomfortable feeling to be running with the herd—no matter the true value of the index you are buying. The fact that it feels uncomfortable will help make you more successful.

Often when you invest in success, there will be a dip. The next time you run your screen, you will be forced to sell. Once you sell, the index will often run back up. Don't look back, regardless of whether it goes higher or drops back down. You are following a system that is not designed or intended to milk every last price or get off exactly at the top. That is fairyland. This is the real world. And this system really works.

# 12

## Hedge for All the Right Reasons: Uncorrelated/Hedge

### CHAPTER NOTES

1. An uncorrelated asset is one that could move either with or against the market.
2. Uncorrelated asset classes could be structured within a portfolio as a "shield" or a "sword." They can work to reduce portfolio risk or, in fact, increase risk—and the potential return.
3. The term *hedge* is another way of defining an uncorrelated investment strategy.
4. A hedging strategy is quite different from a hedge fund.
5. Hedging is an important component of a Personal Pounce Platform.

The purpose of this chapter is to define what hedging really is and to discuss what it can do for your portfolio. We will design a portion of your portfolio, System 3, that is not directly correlated, or move in tandem, with the benchmark. It may even move in the opposite direction. You will be exposed to a handful of investment strategies using uncorrelated assets.

You may be looking to Pounce down on a bubble, create a pair trade, create a Market Neutral strategy, or invest in a Fallen Angel. The specific investment strategy that you use will be decided based on the direction of the market and the outcome of your P3 indicators.

Anytime you turn on CNBC, you're bound to hear someone discussing hedges. Industry buzzwords like this are often used without good definitions, leaving the observer a bit lost. Are hedges good? Do I need some? What will they do for me?

First off, don't confuse a hedge with a hedge fund. Often vilified (due to some spectacular and well-publicized blowups), hedge funds are private investment partnerships that may or may not engage in hedging. The word *hedge* is used because, in the early days of hedge funds, almost all of them engaged in some type of hedging. Even though that's no longer the case, the name stuck.

Hedges are investments made to reduce the risk of another investment while still allowing for some profit from the original investment. Hedges can take any number of forms. One common type is what's called a pairs trade, where the trader doesn't really have an opinion as to where the market is going but does think that a particular stock is inexpensive relative to some other stock, often within the same industry. For instance, perhaps you believe that Abercrombie & Fitch's stock has not necessarily performed well. But your research shows Abercrombie has excellent growth and a terrific brand, and is trading at a better valuation than competitor Urban Outfitters (all this is hypothetical). You could buy Abercrombie and sell short (basically make a bet against) Urban Outfitters in the belief that Abercrombie is a relatively good deal.

Should Urban rise, the argument is the entire sector is rising, so Abercrombie should go up even higher than Urban. If Urban drops, Abercrombie should not drop as much. At the end of the day (or, realistically, the end of the month), the objective is to settle your loss and realize your gains. The next spread should, hypothetically, be net positive. This strategy is often used as a risk-averse strategy and is what is known as Market Neutral.

For the purpose of discussion, let's focus on the strategy for hedging and not on hedge funds. As I say, they have been vilified for some high-profile blowups. Hedge funds are a low-regulated industry, if they are regulated at all. Your irrational rational brain associates hedge funds with big players making big money. And if you can get in, do so. However, many of the highly respected managers know their limitations and either close their funds to new investors or make minimums so high that only a select few can participate.

Hedging isn't limited to traders, though. Some of the most prolific hedgers are firms that you work with every day. The airline you fly most likely buys futures, or contracts as a hedge against higher fuel prices. They attempt to "lock in" fuel prices so they won't get stuck with higher bills if fuel prices go up. The company that makes your shampoo probably sells that same shampoo in Mexico and they probably hedge the peso versus the dollar, knowing that they'll be getting paid in pesos and will have to convert them. Farmers are known for hedging the prices of their crops—by selling futures at the beginning of their growing season, they are able to lock in the price that they will obtain for their crop at the end of the season, regardless of what the corn market has done in between.

## POUNCE ON THE BUY WRITE:
## THE LAZY PREDATOR'S PERFECT OPTION

*Strategy 1: Hedge Investment.* For the average investor, the most frequently used hedge is the purchase or sale of options. In fact, even if they don't know the first thing about trading options, it's not uncommon for the folks that manage mutual funds to use options to hedge, so it's quite possible you have hedged positions within funds you own and don't even know it.

As a primer, options are contracts that allow the buyer the right, but do not impose the obligation, to buy or sell a stock at a specified price, on or before a specified date. An option that allows the buyer to buy a stock is known as a *call option*, and one that allows the buyer to sell a stock is known as a *put*. The amount that the buyer pays to the seller for this right is known as the *premium*. Options can be quite complicated, so, if option-related strategy is something that you're interested in pursuing, find an expert who can help you.

Options are typically used as hedges in two different ways—as a *covered call* strategy or a *protective put* strategy. The covered call allows the owners of a stock to draw some additional income by selling someone else the right to buy stock from them. Assume that you have 100 shares of ABC, which are trading at $50. You could sell someone a call with a $55 strike price for some premium (let's say $1 per share, for the purposes of this example), with three months in which the other party can exercise it. If ABC is trading at or above $55 at the end of that period, you'll most likely be obligated to sell your stock to the other party for $55, even if ABC is now trading at $60. Your "true" sales price, though, is the $55 plus the $1 in premium you received for a total of $56. If ABC is trading below $55, the option expires "worthless" and you get to

keep the $1. Broken down, your hedge is using the additional in-
come to cushion the potential losses, but giving up some upside in
the stock as a trade-off.

The protective put strategy is almost exactly the opposite of the
covered call strategy. Again, you start by owning the stock, but, instead of selling someone else the right to buy the stock from you,
you are buying the right from the other party to force the other
party to buy the stock from you if it goes below a certain point.
For example, assume again that you own 100 shares of ABC, trading at $50. You could buy a put with a $45 strike price (which we
will again assume is trading at $1 per share); this would allow you
to sell the stock to the other party for $45 any time between now
and expiration. If the stock is trading at $30 at expiration, you got
a good deal, with a net sales price of $44 per share ($45 strike, less
$1 premium paid for the put). If the stock is trading above $45 at
expiration, the put expires worthless and you keep your stock, but
you have essentially added an extra $1 to your basis price. Just as
you pay your premium for car insurance, you buy an insurance
policy, but you don't have to file a claim.

The question, then, is: Do these hedges really work? Do they
add a level of protection against a market that may be moving in
another direction? If so, how much is that protection worth? The
answer is really on a case-by-case basis—receiving the premium
for selling a covered call doesn't really help out much if it means
that you held a stock that drops 20 percent in value, just as buying
a protective put doesn't end up being worth much if the stock you
are holding goes up 20 percent. What's interesting, though, are the
results attributed to the BuyWrite indexes published by the
Chicago Board Options Exchange (CBOE). (A buy-write is another

name for a covered call.) The CBOE publishes the performance of their S&P 500 BuyWrite Index under the symbol "BXM." From the time that they began tracking it, in June 1988, until March 2006, BXM had an annualized return of 11.84 percent versus 11.76 percent for the S&P 500 Total Return Index. Despite a marginally better return than the underlying index, where BXM really shines is volatility. The Standard Deviation of Monthly Returns during that period was 9.4 percent for the BuyWrite Index versus 14.0 percent for the Total Return Index.

Several independent studies have confirmed that this strategy in fact would have been a prudent diversification technique due to a much lower deviation than that of the Standard & Poor's 500 Index.

As a Pounce investor, you already know why something of this nature is favored: It is passive. It simply takes the emotions out of trying to choose which investment to make.

This concept really should have you sitting up straight and taking notice. Instead of you trying to create complicated option strategies, you could buy one security that does it for you, an index of covered calls. You do very little work, and the goal is to simply crank ahead using this strategy.

### When to Use the BuyWrite

The BuyWrite could be a consistent strategy within System 3 of Pounce. In fact, I would highly encourage you to research the possibility of investing 5 percent to 10 percent of your System 3 funds in this or a similar index of covered calls and leave it.

If the P3 indicators are heading lower, I like the strategy even more. During rising P3 environments and bull markets, the returns in a covered call strategy will be capped. If you are comfortable with your P3 indicators, through the ease of buying and selling through BuyWrite, you could sell as your P3 indicators give you a strong Pounce signal. As the indicators show a top or a contraction, increase your BuyWrite exposure.

*Strategy 2: Ultra Shorts and Bear Funds.* Ultra Shorts and bear funds are to be used only when your P3 indicators are showing clear signs that the market, sectors, or stocks are in bubble territory and peaking. Even if you see a peak forming, the risk is so great that you should wait until the trend is confirmed, which would mean you would not likely invest until the sector begins to fall.

Ultra Shorts are ETFs that bet a certain sector or market will drop in value. They are either aggressive or very aggressive. Some Ultra Short funds will use enough leverage so that if a certain market drops, their fund will receive double the appreciation. If you invest in an Ultra Short S&P ETF and the market drops 10 percent, the fund is designed to appreciate 20 percent. The flip side is true as well. If the S&P rises in value 10 percent, this fund could lose 20 percent.

Ultra Short and bear funds are not to be held for long periods of time. Remember, most bear markets last less than one year, and chances are you will invest only after the trend turns negative.

Review these holdings every month during your Pounce meeting. After two months of a reversing trend on two of your P3 Indicators, it's time to get out. Two months is usually not long enough to truly determine if the trend is broken, but remember, all you are attempting to do is make a decent return on the uncorrelated assets, to offset the short-term losses that may occur in your Core strategy.

There are very few solid bear market mutual funds. To find one, search the appropriate sites—lipperweb.com, morningstar.com—read the analysts' reports, concern yourself with the amount of leverage, and make a decision. Make sure you ask if you are penalized or will be charged an extra fee for trading in and out of the fund within a certain period of time.

The same is true for ETFs that short markets. Read the prospectus, tear sheets, and any other material you can find to make a determination that is right for you.

*Strategy 3: Market Neutral.* This strategy is designed for all markets. However, I use it most in markets that are not doing much of anything, and in down markets.

Using my P3 indicators, I am looking for neutral readings—neutral to heading lower. This being said, please know that there is nothing wrong with using Market Neutral during up markets as well. It offers an excellent hedge, and, similar to the BuyWrite, could be a consistent holding in your System 3.

It is truly hard to find a Market Neutral fund. A Market Neutral fund is one that buys the same number of stocks as it sells. Further, it will match the same number of stocks it buys and sells for each industry. On the surface a Market Neutral concept seems like a strategy that can't make up its mind. It is very difficult to discipline yourself to know that through up and down markets you will be both buying and selling the exact number of securities in each sector. It's hard because you *know* technology is going higher, so you should have more longs in this sector, and more shorts in energy.

Market Neutral is a strategy to "never lose money." It is not designed for growth; it is designed for principal preservation.

Let's assume you have found a system that is fairly reliable at searching out undervalued stocks. Perhaps you create a search that filters out stocks with earnings that have exceeded the benchmark for three years and is projected to exceed the benchmark during the next year. However, you weed out any stocks that have a price-to-earnings ratio that is greater than the current and expected growth rate. Finally, only those stocks that have a price-to-sales ratio of less than 1.5 can be included in your "buy list." I like this list; it is a great value/growth screen and has a fairly good shot at beating the market. Conversely, you say, those stocks that have negative earnings growth, exceedingly high price to earnings and price to sales, would probably perform worse than the market. This would be your "sell list."

The concept now would be to match the stocks in each sector with equal numbers of buys and equal numbers of shorts. Run your screen once per month to "rebalance."

At the end of the day, what your Market Neutral fund should deliver is that in a down market the stocks you shorted will go down more than the market, and the stocks you bought should go down less than the market. The net result is an intended modest gain. The same scenario is reversed in an up market. In a market that is not doing much of anything, this strategy would probably offer the best absolute value.

I realize that this strategy may be a bit expensive to implement on your own. Trading fees could be high. This strategy would require possibly 100 buys, so 100 sells. If you find that scary, consider researching Market Neutral funds.

*Strategy 4: Modified Market Neutral.* This strategy has proven effective through all markets: bulls, bears, peaks, and Void. If a Market Neutral is a fund that truly seeks to not lose money, a long-short fund is Market Neutral's wild brother. A true long-short fund will do whatever possible to make money. A long-short could be 100 percent long, or borrow money on margin to go short on certain securities. Although the potential upside is huge, the downside is huge as well. If the buys do not produce a profit, and the sells don't produce a profit, added to the borrowing costs, losses could mount fast.

To this end, I propose a modified Market Neutral/long-short strategy. This is one that seeks to be 50 percent long and 50 percent short at any time. However, if the screen that you build does not yield any potential buys in a particular sector, you do not have to match stock for stock in each sector. And if your screen does not yield any particular shorts in that sector, you do not have to short any stocks in that sector. The result is not a true Market Neutral wherein you are buying an equal number of stocks in each sector. But in the macro you are buying and selling equal percentages.

Logically, this system makes sense to me. As we have already discussed, during any market certain sectors head higher, while others move lower. I want to buy those headed higher, and sell those headed lower.

The result is a beefed-up Market Neutral, or a watered-down long short. Let's just call it the Ken Special. Does it work? Glad you asked. I'll build a Ken Special just for you.

## KEN SPECIAL

The strategy, like everything I attempt, is very simple. I screened:

**BUY:**
- ✓ Price-to-sales ratio between 1 and 2.1
- ✓ Market value greater than $1 billion
- ✓ Price >10
- ✓ % change in EPS this quarter vs. same quarter last year > 0
- ✓ Earnings surprise greater than 35 percent
- ✓ Relative strength >1

**SELL:**
- ✓ P/S > 2.1
- ✓ % change in EPS this quarter vs. same quarter last year < 0
- ✓ Earnings surprise is 0 or below 0
- ✓ Did not screen for relative strength
- ✓ Market value greater than $1 billion
- ✓ Price > 10

Notice how this simple screen incorporates Investment Psyche (relative strength), with the rest of the parameters being valuation criteria.

If you created a hypothetical model using the simple components of this strategy, hypothetical back-testing suggests the strategy would have performed quite well against the Standard & Poor's 500 Index. During this isolated experiment, I reran the screen every month for the hypothetical back-test. The turnover was not as high as one would expect (meaning many stocks made the list several months in a row), but the hypothetical return wowed us!

Remember that back-testing is not a pure science, and past performance is absolutely no guarantee of future results.

**And this is the result:**

### Modified Market Neutral—The Results

| | |
|---|---|
| Total positive return periods | 19 |
| Strategy total return (modified Market Neutral) | 13% |
| S&P 500 return | 3.10% |
| Number of periods it beat S&P | 10 |
| Standard deviation of returns | 1.50% |
| Standard deviation for S&P 500 | 3.93% |

*Strategy 5: Pair Trade.* The pair trade is a stable hedge strategy and should be used through all markets: bull, bear, peaks, and Void.

The concept of a pair trade is similar to both a Market Neutral concept and a long short concept. In essence, you determine which asset class is overvalued, and short that index (or buy a short ETF) and find the undervalued sector that should benefit from a sell-off of the overvalued sector. You go long in that undervalued sector.

For example, let's assume that, based on your P3 indicators, you believe energy is expensive, and the indicators point to a peak, or perhaps it already began to sell off. The high cost of energy has been the cause, in part, of other sectors performing poorly. Assume, for example, that high energy prices have aided the economic slow-down. Since more money goes to fill up your tank, less money is available for discretionary purposes. The discretionary sector has sold off dramatically and is considered undervalued based on the P3 indicators, and poised for a rebound. Or, it may already have begun to rebound.

Notice that, since March 2007, the discretionary sector has dropped in value, while energy (XLE) has soared. Recall that I stated that one leading indicator of an economic slowdown is discretionary stocks selling off. Isn't it interesting that this sector started selling off in March 2007, two quarters before the economy began to sell off?

### News Flash Update

In the preceding graph, the data ends in May 2008. Well, when I had a chance to make edits for this book, I decided to update the graph. Look at what happened through mid-July:

What happened was that SPECS started coming up and the oil bubble burst! I love it when a good plan comes together.

Special Consm Serv vs. SPDR Energy Index
July 21, 2006-July 17, 2008

*Strategy 6: Fallen Angels.* This strategy is best used when there are neutral or bearish indicators. Basically, you want to catch the market before the next upturn. Fallen Angels does not do as well during peak or falling markets.

Read the title of this section. I don't want a "falling" angel. That would imply that it is still falling. I want a Fallen Angel. I want a great company, on sale, that is ripe for pouncing.

When do situations like this occur? Please remember, I am not politically correct. I am revealing myself to you as an investment predator. I do not ever wish harm or negativity to befall anyone. However, I also need profits. Give me bad news: an act of God, freak occurrences, a recession, a bear market. I'll give you a Fallen Angel.

How is a Fallen Angel different from a Rising Star? Something happened to cause a hiccup. Something is not perfect in the world. Rising Stars are shining bright, they have not stumbled as of yet. Eventually a Rising Star will fall. You will have to decide whether that company is either a Fallen Angel or a forgettable company.

A Fallen Angel has an excellent probability for stock apprecia-tion. It has increased earnings or sales forecasts, the valuation is much less expensive than its historical value, and most likely the market as a whole is starting to show positive Investment Psyche/Market Be-havior. The Economic variables do not play as large as a role in a Fallen Angel (they have already seen their recession, of sorts). Fallen Angels fit into your System 3: Hedge Pounce Portfolio. When the economy is bright green and too optimistic, you will have fewer Fallen Angels and more hedges. When the economy is yellow with down arrows, you want both hedges and Fallen Angels (provided the Investment Psyche is positive to back you up). When the econ-omy is red, you want Fallen Angels.

Fallen Angels are created when:

1. A natural or man-made disaster occurs
2. One-time negative events hit a company or sector
3. There are bear markets and recessions
4. Overvaluation or earning misses occur, causing the herd to "leave the party"
5. Another stock or market in general went down, and this stock went down in sympathy—the *no fault way* (the saying "throwing the baby out with the bathwater" comes to mind)

Before you can truly know if you have a Fallen Angel or just a cheap stock, ask a few of these questions:

1. What was the company's reaction to the stock sell-off? If the company sold off, and is now cheaper than its historic aver-

ages, put it on your radar and see what happens to the stock and the earnings after their next quarterly report.

2. What are the sales doing throughout this period? Are they still going higher, or did they simply have a one- or two-quarter miss? That is a characteristic of a Fallen Angel, not a cheap stock.

3. Did the company lose market share? This is a cheap stock characteristic.

4. Verify that Investor Psyche has bottomed out (readings can and will be low, but not gapping down any longer).

As with any of the strategies, you can find Fallen Angels in all sorts of places. I'll let you in on a little secret: Fallen Angels are really another version of growth, but at very reasonable prices . . . almost—can I say it?—deep value!

Of course, you can create any screen you like. This is a variation of a screen that I prefer:

### FALLEN ANGEL SCREEN

1. P/E $\leq$ 80% of the industry median and $\leq$ 14
2. P/S $\leq$ 1.5
3. Market cap $\geq$ $1 billion
4. % change in the next quarter estimates $> 0$

### Cheap Stocks

Some people thought Kmart was cheap—right before it filed for bankruptcy and the shareholders lost their money. Krispy Kreme was once a Rising Star, and then it was a Shooting Star. Is it a Fallen Angel today? No. Perhaps bottom feeders will make money with it, but it is not and will not be a Fallen Angel until the company is "quality." They need to have profits, they need to reduce their debt, and they need cash flow. Again, Krispy Kreme is a great brand and perhaps an opportunity for someone, just not you.

## KRISPY KREME

From the moment this company went public it was a classic bubble in the making. Krispy Kreme was the "craze" *du jour*. Everyone from big Hollywood stars to Joe next door had to have one. Come on, they made donuts! The stock was at $50 per share at one point. And then came (gasp in surprise) their first earning miss. It didn't take long for the herd to exit stage left!

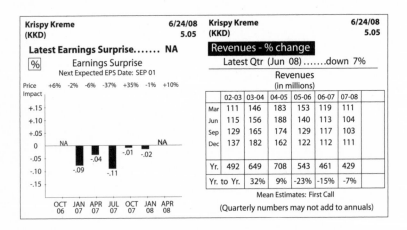

| Krispy Kreme<br>(KKD) | | 6/24/08<br>5.05 |
| --- | --- | --- |

**Latest Earnings Surprise....... NA**

| Price<br>Impact | +6% | -2% | -6% | -37% | +35% | -1% | +10% |
| --- | --- | --- | --- | --- | --- | --- | --- |

Earnings Surprise
Next Expected EPS Date: SEP 01

Values: NA, -.09, -.04, -.11, -.01, -.02, NA

OCT 06, JAN 07, APR 07, JUL 07, OCT 07, JAN 08, APR 08

**Revenues - % change**
Latest Qtr (Jun 08) .......down 7%

Revenues (in millions)

| | 02-03 | 03-04 | 04-05 | 05-06 | 06-07 | 07-08 | |
| --- | --- | --- | --- | --- | --- | --- | --- |
| Mar | 111 | 146 | 183 | 153 | 119 | 111 | |
| Jun | 115 | 156 | 188 | 140 | 113 | 104 | |
| Sep | 129 | 165 | 174 | 129 | 117 | 103 | |
| Dec | 137 | 182 | 162 | 122 | 112 | 111 | |
| Yr. | 492 | 649 | 708 | 543 | 461 | 429 | |
| Yr. to Yr. | | 32% | 9% | -23% | -15% | -7% | |

Mean Estimates: First Call
(Quarterly numbers may not add to annuals)

It still shows earnings misses and decelerating revenue. This is not yet a Fallen Angel. However, it is worth watching, as a trend is forming with lower misses and lower negative revenue.

## CASE HISTORY OF A RECENT
## FALLEN ANGEL: MCDONALD'S

Remember the stock market dip in 2003? You had a perfect storm: weakness at McDonald's, a recession, and a bear market. But what perhaps you didn't take into account is this Fallen Angel dropped significantly below what it usually traded at as compared to its earnings.

January 2003 was a bad month for the McDonald's Corporation. The stock had been steadily declining with the bad market, soft same store sales, and poor global sentiment for the United States as we threatened to invade Iraq. But in January, McDonald's shocked Wall Street by issuing its first-ever quarterly loss.

With the bleak report and tough prospects, you can imagine what the analysts did—tore it apart, of course. And the herd exited stage right. A cheap stock became much cheaper. But then the CEO was credited with "revitalizing the stores." He made improvements in the menus, the toilets, and much more.

The stock started to rise and then, tragedy—McDonald's chairman and CEO James Cantalupo died suddenly of a heart attack. Charlie Bell, 44, replaced Cantalupo, and one month after ascending to his new rank he was diagnosed with cancer. Bell died less than one year later.

The question is, Did the stock price justify the negativity? In hindsight it is easy to say, no, but the reality is, we didn't know what changes were about to take place. The McDonald's Corporation overhauled the menu by introducing new salads and yogurt parfaits, improving coffee in an effort to compete with Starbucks, and aligning their advertising with the target market. We didn't see any of it coming. And we never will.

After the stock started its turnaround you had Investor Psyche that turned from neutral to slightly positive; extremely favorable valuation; an economy migrating higher from trough to peak; store sales moving higher; earnings and sales in general moving higher. You didn't need to know the future. This story occurs every day: from McDonald's to Wal-Mart, from Hewlett-Packard to U.S. Steel. All you needed was to trust in the Power of 3.

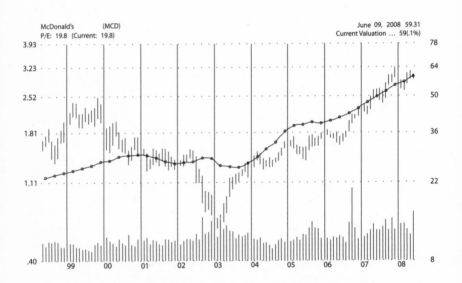

## DO WE POUNCE ON THE FINANCIAL SECTOR?
## IS THIS A FALLEN ANGEL?

My best guess would say it is time, after such a terrible performance for such an extended period, to pounce on financials. So, are they a Fallen Angel?

This is a great study. Financial stocks have fallen off a cliff. Yet selling persists. Look at the heavy volume to this downside action. And this is even after one of the worst sell-offs the financial sector has experienced. Investment Psyche has almost reached "red," or extreme selling. In fact, RSI has almost dropped to extreme

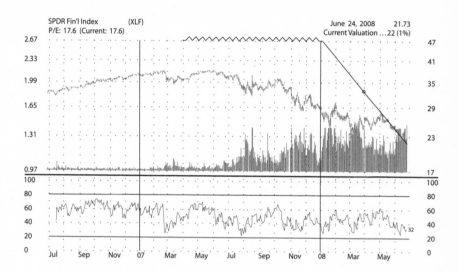

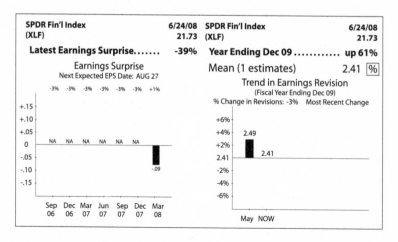

pessimism as well. If Economy is red, and Market Value is fair to undervalued it would be a Fallen Angel—and probably will be soon. But wait until the indicator comes to you, lest you catch a falling knife. If the trend is reversed and the Investment Psyche quickly turns positive at the same time the economy is red or trends upward, you now evaluate it as a Rising Star. In the graph on page 243, notice that the RSI is still negative. You do not need to wait for a three-month confirmation; two months of ascending RSI and analysts' earnings per share estimates being upgraded would be sufficient.

## ONE MORE FALLEN ANGEL

### Food Distributor: Positive Pounce

All this talk of inflation, high energy prices, higher crop prices, and food for fuel must have taken a toll on food distributors. The sector has been bruised and battered. The chart line, however, shows continued growth of earnings. Perhaps the herd overdid it. When the selling started, the Angel fell pretty hard, piercing the earnings trendline.

Future growth projections have been revised higher; earnings surprises have been positive as well. You could look for the individual stocks in this sector; however, why take the individual stock risk? If the sector is showing positive signs, playing the sector could offer much of the upside without the individual stock downside.

## ONE MORE EXAMPLE:
## THIS FALLEN ANGEL IS NOT QUITE READY

A Fallen Angel may possess the proper economic environment and
be positioned well from a valuation standpoint. But if the herd has

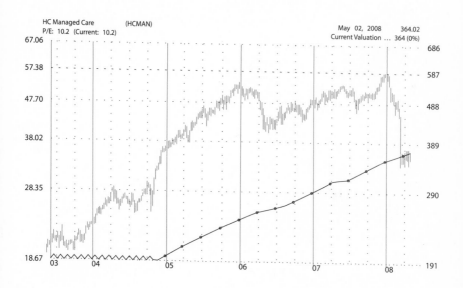

HC Managed Care          (HCMAN)
P/E: 10.2 (Current: 10.2)

May 02, 2008    364.02
Current Valuation ... 364 (0%)

| HC - Managed Care | 6/24/08 |
| (HCMAN) | 312.81 |

P/E
Trailing P/E Ratio .. ............... .8.7
Forward P/E Ratio .................8.3

Dividend Yield ......... ............1%

Earnings Per Share - % change
  Latest Qtr (Mar 08)............ ....up 6%
  Latest 12 Months ............. ...up 18%
  5-Year Hist. Growth Rate ............21%

Estimated Earnings - First Call

| HC - Managed Care | 6/24/08 |
| (HCMAN) | 312.81 |

**Earnings Per Share - % change**  2.6
Latest Qtr (Mar 08) .. ............up 6%
Earnings - 4-Quarter Moving Average
5 Yr Hist Growth Rate: 21%
Long Term Future Growth Rate: 15%

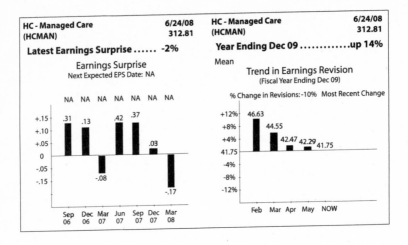

been bloodied and the damage is fresh, this meat is rotten. Wait for another day.

The health care industry is one of my favorite macroeconomic trend stories. However, the managed care section, as cheap as it looks, has not seen enough of a trend reversal to get positive yet. If earnings are still showing a downtrend, it really doesn't matter how cheap the company appears.

I'll even argue that the sector looks cheap.

So what happened? Here is the culprit. Negative earnings surprise, downward revision. It appears cheap according to Valuation. Maybe the P/E is low and maybe the growth is good. But if earnings are being revised downward, it's still dead money. Before you buy it you should wait until revisions are a bit higher in order to eliminate unwanted risk. If you are a deep-value player, I would suggest that the value looks great. But, for us to consider this a Fallen Angel, you need a positive earnings trend, not a negative one.

## SUMMARY

Congratulations. You now possess six advanced Uncorrelated/ Hedge strategies. These big strategies are probably nothing like what you have ever been exposed to. If you used them properly in conjunction with the P3 indicators and inside of System 3 of your Personal Pounce Platform, you will be the Pounce King (or Queen).

# 13

## Personal Pounce Platform

### CHAPTER NOTES

1. Rule Number One—the most important investment system is to have a system. To this end, create a Personal Pounce investment Platform.
2. Rule Number Two—don't outsmart your system. Adhere to your system as it is created.
3. Rule Number Three—don't lose money. I know that sounds basic enough, but it's true. Most solid returns are lost by allowing your investment gains or principal to erode. This speaks to your sell discipline.
4. Rule Number Four—keep it simple!
5. The Personal Pounce Platform will consist of three systems, each centered on a specific and tangible investment strategy.
6. System 1, Core, is designed to benchmark against the S&P. You will create a core portfolio of between twenty-five and

thirty-five stocks and manage your system once—and only once—per month. Most of the stocks within this system are designed to be part of the Rising Stars and Pounce for Income and Growth investment strategies.

7. System 2, Tactical, focuses on investing in leaders. It is your Top Gun!

8. System 3, Uncorrelated or Hedge, relies on assets that tend to move in a different direction than the overall market, or which have virtually no movement. These could include Fallen Angels, cash, Market Neutral, Pair Trade, etc.

9. Tune out all the pitches, hype, and greed that will deflect you from your singular focus—which is adding alpha and absolute wealth. Do not concern yourself with what your friend, your neighbor, or your father is doing with his investments.

10. Now that you will be required to spend less time on subjective decisions, and less time worrying what the news of the day is, enjoy the ride.

It's time to put it all together.

Your Personal Pounce Platform is designed to take advantage of all markets: up, down, peak, or flat. Using P3, you will ascertain the direction of the market: Either we are moving from fair value to overvalued or we are moving from fair value to undervalued. We are either at a peak or at the bottom of the trough.

1. Don't chase your opponent. Simply wait him out. In a fight, even if the guy can hit harder than you, if you can tire him

out, pretty soon—when you are fresh and ready—you can start picking away at him. Your opponent is too tired to do anything about it. When you set up to create your System 1: Core, you will not be chasing high-flying stocks or bubbles. You will strengthen your core by allowing into your model only those companies that offer superior growth potential at reasonable prices. When something goes wrong, you will shed the company from your portfolio like burning away unwanted fat. When a specific holding grows too big and too expensive, you will shed yet again, and revert to your center, your core.

2. Use speed and tactical ability. If you are fighting a giant, your best chance is to use your speed and tactical ability to get inside, take a chunk of flesh, and get out before the giant pounces on you! In your System 2: Tactical, you will engage the biggest companies—not biggest in terms of size, but those that have the biggest upside potential based on their earnings and sales. You will get in, take some flesh (profits), and try to get out before they crash down.

3. You are going to learn the art of Jujitsu. Jujitsu is like a chess match: Opponents use each other as their own weakness. One uses the other's momentum and mistakes as an advantage to win the fight. This is the portion that you counter. You hedge, and you rebalance. System 3 is the portion of your platform designed to negatively correlate the rest of the portfolio: to counterattack; to pounce down on bubbles.

| System 1 | System 2 | System 3 |
|---|---|---|
| Core—Rising Stars/ Pounce for Income and Growth | Tactical/Top Gun | Uncorrelated/Hedge |
| 25–35 Target Holdings | 6 Target Holdings | 6 Target Strategies (Use 4–6 at any given time) |
| **Total: 35–47 Target Holdings** | | |

## USE YOUR NEWFOUND SKILLS

Finally, you possess the tools necessary for absolute wealth. You are an Investment Predator: trained, conditioned, and predisposed to build wealth with, through, and because of, adverse conditions—not in spite of them.

Think about it: Prior to this, you had a ready, fire, aim type of strategy. Through irrational rationalization you fired. And what you readied your sights at were companies that probably did not fit either; your personal investment platform (alpha model), or a proper investment strategy that stacked the odds of winning on your behalf.

Now that you have steadied your mind and learned the proper methods for determining where we are in the cacophony of the market, you can create your Personal Pounce Platform.

**Ready . . .**

Being ready is training your brain to focus on the data you require, and only this data. Relate all investment options to your platform, with the goal being to minimize outside noise, greed, and irrational rationalization of what doesn't matter.

**Aim . . .**

You have a clear target. You possess the P3 indicators designed to help you peg the direction of the market. Your directional guide is clear, focused, and tangible.

Further, look at all of the investment strategies you have learned: bubble strategies and pair trades; Rising Stars, Shooting Stars, and Fallen Angels; hedge strategies and income strategies. Load it up, and let's Pounce.

**Pounce!**

Preparation is 99 percent of success. Be sure that you are now prepared to pounce. To pounce, we need the last bit of information—the missing link, if you will. The Personal Pounce Platform is that link.

The objective of the Personal Pounce Platform is to provide a system that is easy to research, administer, and implement and in which you can grow and prosper through all markets, chaotic environments, and uncertain periods. The strategies and concepts are to provide you with a focus, not a black box. This is not simple math. It is not absolute. We create a system, we support the system, and, through this discipline, following the trends, we will achieve the greatness we seek.

## CREATE AN INVESTMENT PLATFORM STATEMENT

Sample: *"The Stern Family Personal Pounce Platform is created to provide absolute investment returns."*

As mundane and worthless as this may seem, you will see how helpful creating your own personal statement is and will be. When you are in doubt, it guides you. When you are set to make an impulsive decision, it guides you. As the saying goes, "Before you can score, you must first have a goal."

This goal will be achieved through strict adherence to the three investment systems selected and implemented.

I will begin by allocating 33 percent of my risk capital to each of the three investment systems. As each of the three systems strays from the original 33 percent allocation, I will seek to rebalance on a systematic basis to maintain a targeted 33 percent allocation. Every year, I will sell sufficient assets to bring the level of any system that has grown in excess of 33 percent back to 33 percent, placing the proceeds with the system that is under the 33 percent goal.

The final goal of the Personal Pounce Platform is to maximize absolute wealth, mitigate any unnecessary fees and expenses, and

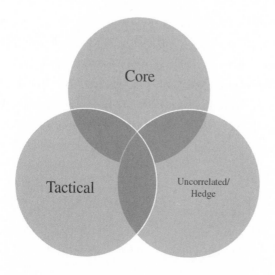

maintain tax efficiently whenever possible. Here's the chart again from chapter 1:

| Core | Tactical | Uncorrelated/Hedge |
|---|---|---|
| System 1 | System 2 | System 3 |
| • Rising Stars<br>• Pounce for Income and Growth | • Top Gun | • Fallen Angel<br>• BuyWrite<br>• Market Neutral<br>• Modified Market Neutral<br>• Pair Trade<br>• Ultra Short |

## IMPLEMENT THE MONTHLY POUNCE MEETING

Consistent with all the teachings in *Pounce*, the Personal Pounce Platform is designed to remove quick-trigger reactions due to "stories of the day." It is also created to take three different approaches to the market, with a goal being adding within and creating absolute wealth. One last goal is to keep your life simple. Meeting once per month is simple. The maximum number of strategies that your Personal Pounce Platform will utilize at any time is nine. That's it—nine strategies! In Core you have two: Rising Stars and Pounce for Income and Growth. In Tactical, you have three Top Guns: Top Gun for S&P 500 Sectors, Top Gun for Market Cap and Value Sectors, and Top Gun for Global. Finally, in your Uncorrelated/Hedge portfolio, you will deploy preferably four or six strategies at any one time. Assume the bias is bullish. You will utilize Pair Trade, Fallen Angels, BuyWrite, and Modified Market Neutral. Nine. That's it.

A key part of the process prevents you from trading or buying and selling based on whenever you feel it is appropriate. Rather, you must choose a set day each month to make any necessary buy and sell. You can do research leading up to this moment, but regardless of how panicky you are during the month over a certain situation, you can't sell. No matter how excited you are about another potential acquisition, you can't invest until that fateful day once per month.

Please consider the following as a sample fixed agenda.

## MONTHLY POUNCE AGENDA

1. Create twelve months' worth of agendas noting which activities are monthly, which are quarterly, and which are annual.
   a. Monthly: Rising Star, Pair Trade, Market Neutral and Modified Market Neutral, Ultra Short.
   b. Quarterly: Pounce for Income and Growth (PIG) and Top Gun are traded once per quarter.
   c. Quarterly: the Pounce Platform is retested to determine bullish, bearish, or neutral (Void) stance.
   d. Annually: the Pounce Platform is rebalanced back to ⅓, ⅓, ⅓ in each system. If your System 1: Core has more than 33 percent, you would sell a sufficient amount to get it back to 33 percent. Place the proceeds from the sales into the strategy that is at less than 33 percent.

2. Review the P3 indicators in an effort to determine if the Pounce Platform will be changed, at the next opportunity, to a different bias: bullish, bearish, or neutral. Remember that you cannot change the bias more often than every three months. Further, the bias can only be changed if the

P3 indicators indicated the new bias in the last two (out of the last three) meetings. As an example: If P3 states that the stance is bearish, this has to have been true for the last two monthly Pounce meetings. If you had changed the bias the previous month, and the P3 indicators change the subsequent month and maintain this change over the next two months, but reverse to another bias in the third month (the month you were able to make the change), you would be precluded from making the change. The indicators must have read the same for the last two months in order for you to be able to change the bias.

3. System 1: Core
    a. Rising Stars screen is run every month. Depending on the Pounce bias—bullish, bearish, or neutral—you will be clear as to how to allocate the result of the investment candidates that the screens reveal.
    b. Pounce for Income and Growth is run every quarter. Again, depending on the Personal Pounce Platform bias, you will know how to allocate.

4. System 2: Tactical/Top Gun
    a. You have three asset classes and leaders. You are investing in the Top Gun in each sector.
    b. Review this every quarter.
    c. It is best to start these on different quarter intervals so that you may make a trade every quarter except one. Do asset classes in January. In March you can do S&P sectors; in June, begin global. Once you have the setup, these

screens are run once per quarter. By staggering the quarters, it evens out the trading patterns.

    **d.** This strategy is repeated regardless of the P3 indicators.

**5.** System 3: Uncorrelated/Hedge

    **a.** You have six arrows in your quiver. Six uncorrelated and/or hedge strategies. These strategies will be rotated based on the Pounce Platform bias.

    **b.** Most of the investment strategies with System 3 are monthly. Run the proper investment screens monthly.

## SYSTEM 1: CORE

Much discussion and work has centered on indexes such as the S&P 500. It is a widely followed index because it is just that—wide. With 500 stocks, it represents a fairly large universe (keep in mind, however, that the weight for each stock in the index is based on the size or market capitalization of the company). In contrast, the Dow Jones Industrial Average is comprised of only thirty stocks. This index has performed exceptionally well. The bottom line is that too many stocks lead to overdiversification. If you own too many stocks on one index, you are, likely, in effect, creating a closet index fund. Overdiversification (buying too many stocks on one index) can make it more difficult to "beat the index" or add positive alpha.

Your Core system should compare to the S&P 500. However, the screen that we have developed for Rising Stars and Pounce for Income and Growth allows for stocks not included in the Standard & Poor's 500 Index.

The philosophy to System 1: Core is to focus on the stocks with the best value and growth proposition. Our screens attempt to discover those quality companies that offer the best chance for growth at the best price, based on what direction the market is headed. This process of screening will sift out select companies, leaving you with (depending on the market) a core group of stocks.

In aggressive bull markets, the Valuation will probably skew higher as compared with average long-term Valuations. Our models will simply not produce as many stocks. Further, your Personal Pounce Platform will adjust for and accommodate different markets. If the platform is bullish, you can allocate a higher dollar percentage to each stock. Subsequently, in bearish cycles, you would allocate lower percentages. You will see how the Uncorrelated asset classes act as a rudder in varying markets.

**Sector Weightings**

Stocks are often like fish—they move in schools. This is good for you, since you are a pouncing predator. The problem is, many of the stocks may be part of the same sector. Your monthly Rising Stars screen might, for example, produce twenty stocks, but ten stocks would be in the same sector.

This is going to be one of the rare instances that I tell you to make a subjective judgment call. It would be my preference that your portfolio is not weighted too heavily in any one sector. Chances are, if the screen is producing such a high percentage in one sector, you will have enough exposure to this sector in your other investment strategies.

A portfolio skewed toward one sector might provide a very strong return in any given quarter, but the risk far, far exceeds the reward as it relates to core holdings. In the core holding system your portfolio is compared to the S&P 500. The S&P is comprised of ten broad sectors.

However, it would not be advisable to overweight to excess. A 20 percent or greater overweight would be excessive for an initial allocation. Even if this means you had no other stocks to buy (because the screen did not produce any other candidates) and you were forced to sit on some cash, I would prefer this to foolishly overweighting toward one sector.

The sector discussion will be dominated by your valuation screens but should also be reviewed based on the economic cycle. Sectors tend to move (although not exactly) with the economy. Use the following for a general rule of thumb.

## UP AND DOWN LEADERS

A common occurrence is when, by moving right along, you may not realize that danger lurks around the next bend. This is what P3 helps forecast. If a situation develops that everything appears to be going fine, but two of your indicators start to turn negative (say Value is high and Market Behavior is beginning to trend lower), you need to be very careful that the market might be heading lower. In your Core holdings, watch those assets that own stocks in these sectors: consumer discretionary, financials, and technology. First, they may be overvalued, and analysts are too aggressive with their earnings forecasts. Second, when these sectors turn negative, it is often an early warning that the market in general could be headed lower.

### Defensive Sectors

After a recession starts and for the better part of the year following the start date of the recession (remember, the recession will not be called simultaneously to its occurring; you will have to use your judgment to detect signs of it), watch for leadership in health care and consumer staples. These sectors tend to act positively during this period, both from a pure performance standpoint and also to signal the beginning of the end.

## SYSTEM 2: TACTICAL/TOP GUN

After you read chapter 11, you can handle buying leadership. This strategy is objective and requires little thought or change.

In fact, I have found that although it is often down during the bearish and neutral periods, I do not change the strategy with the Personal Pounce Platform bias. Even if the Pounce Platform is bearish, I still follow the strategy. Why? First, because leaders still tend to lead. Second, because I have enough exposure to the Uncorrelated assets that even if I suffer a bit of a loss, I more than make up for it with the gains that I might have missed by selling too early.

It is possible, should you be implementing Tactical based on my first overachiever variation (see chapter 11, page 218), that you are using earnings revisions to discover strength. If no upward earning revisions exist, consider selling your holdings when you are able to (when the three-month hold period is up) and not buying again until revisions are higher. The flaw in this strategy is, however, that revisions do not usually come down until after the stocks fall. So, the strategy is to sell before the earnings are revised downward. And you sell when the sector or asset class begins to weaken—which often happens before the earnings revisions, since stock performance is a leading indicator. Remember, you have three Investment universes we are targeting in this strategy:

Investment Universe 1: Domestic Sectors
Investment Universe 2: Domestic Capital Value and Growth
Investment Universe 3: International Sectors

The sample of ETFs to choose from in this strategy appears on pages 215–16.

## SYSTEM 3: UNCORRELATED/HEDGE

System 3 works as a rudder and an anchor for the other two systems. The Uncorrelated asset classes should be able to provide positive return, positive alpha (a return in excess of the benchmark), through all investment cycles. Recall that Book One showed you an example of earning a low rate of return but suffering no investment losses versus earning a high rate of return with periodic losses. Uncorrelated assets or hedged assets, by their nature, will never earn us a "home run," at least not the way I instruct you to use them. We are not using hedging as a sword, but rather as a shield. For that the goal is consistent returns in all market environments.

It is, of course, possible for one of these strategies—say Fallen Angels—to rise simultaneously with Core or Tactical. That is okay. By slightly altering your criteria you are attacking another aspect of the market.

The intent of System 3 is to discover primarily uncorrelated, consistent, and sometimes out-of-favor investment classes in order to take advantage of mispriced markets.

## Simple Rules

1. Keep it simple but diversified. Do not use more than four investment strategies within System 3 at any one time. (Recall that in the Uncorrelated/Hedge chapter you are exposed to six strategies.) Do not change your strategy, once embarked upon, for at least one year.
2. Rebalance your investment strategies as called for. However, remember that you cannot switch to a new strategy for three months.
3. Pouncing strategies to choose from include:
   CBOE BuyWrite Index
   Fallen Angel
   Pair Trade
   Ultra Short
   Market Neutral
   Modified Market Neutral
4. The P3 must still be used as a guide as to which strategy is used, and within each strategy to choose the specific investment.

## A SIMPLE SYSTEM 3 CHEAT SHEET

*When P3 Shows Bullish.* When Valuation is below historic averages, as it relates to asset classes, markets, and individual investments, I am assuming that something "bad," such as a bear market or a company-specific event, must have happened. Usually if you are able to make the distinction between low Valuations with a positive outlook and low Valuations with a negative outlook, you can find some good opportunities. When Valuation is low with a positive trend, then focus on your macro trends and Fallen Angels, modified Long Shorts, and pair trades. These programs sift out those investment ideas that have a positive outlook.

When Valuation is high, focus on strategies such as Ultra Short, Market Neutral, and pair trades.

During the neutral periods you have a bit more flexibility. However, CBOE BuyWrite Index, Market Neutral, and Fallen Angel are all potential candidates.

## SAMPLE PERSONAL POUNCE PLATFORMS

The bias of your Personal Pounce Platform changes. Remember, you are adding alpha. Alpha is the ability to add value and outperform the market. To do so, the Pounce investor believes in dynamic money management. We are not stagnant and simply willing to watch the markets rise and fall. We seek greatness!

So the Personal Pounce Platform should drift with the bias of the market. As your P3 indicators drift, so, too, should your Personal Pounce Platform.

On page 264 is the key to the P3 indicators that you've already seen. Use this as a guide. Track the indicators every month, but remember that you cannot change the bias of the Personal Pounce Platform any quicker than once per quarter.

I will break from tradition and allow you to use a bit of subjectivity. The P3 indicator will deliver a bias toward bull, bear, or Void. However, if your indicators are showing a very strong trend toward one direction, feel free to slightly modify your PPP toward this trend. Again, just remember that you are forbidden to modify the PPP at a pace of anything greater than once per quarter.

## Bullish

| Core—33% | Tactical—33% | Uncorrelated/Hedge—33% |
|---|---|---|
| 50% Rising Stars | 15% Top Gun S&P 500 | 25% Pair Trade |
| 50% Pounce for Income and Growth | 25% Top Gun Market Capital and Value Indices | 20% Fallen Angels |
| 4% Maximum Weight Per Stock | 60% Top Gun Global | 55% Modified Market Neutral |

## Bearish

| Core—33% | Tactical—33% | Uncorrelated/Hedge—33% |
|---|---|---|
| 50% Rising Star | 10% Top Gun S&P 500 | 20% Pair Trade |
| 50% Pounce for Income and Growth | 25% Top Gun Market Capital Store and Value Indices | 15% CBOE BuyWrite Index |
| 2% Maximum | | 10% Ultra Short |
| Weight—Remaining Goes to Cash | 65% Top Gun Global | 55% Market Neutral |

## Great Void/Neutral

| Core—33% | Tactical—33% | Uncorrelated/Hedge—33% |
|---|---|---|
| 50% Rising Star | 10% Top Gun S&P 500 | 20% Pair Trade |
| 50% Pounce for Income and Growth | 25% Top Gun Market Capital and Value Indices | 15% CBOE BuyWrite Index |
| | | 20% Modified Market Neutral |
| 3% Maximum Weight—Remaining Goes to Cash | 65% Top Gun Global | 45% Market Neutral |

## Pouncing on the Early Bull

When the bull is new, you have a wide array of choices. These choices will be incorporated in your Personal Pounce Platform.

The Pounce investment strategies incorporate all three of the Power indicators and help you sniff out the bull. You will see, for example, that the Rising Stars strategy will identify companies ripe for appreciation.

1. System 1: Core. It is most important to have powerful sales growth and earnings growing and for you to be beating expectations. Early in the bull, valuation, cash flow, and profit margin are less important. You are looking for Rising Stars— these sectors might include technology, discretionary, industrials, materials, and financials, to name a few.

2. System 2: Tactical/Top Gun will be based on the sectors that show strength. However, instead of reviewing these holdings on a quarterly basis as you would in a late bull market, do so semiannually. When leadership is replaced, do not second-guess your Personal Pounce Platform. If one of your holdings after six months is no longer a candidate for your leadership strategy, you have to sell, and not second-guess yourself.

3. This would also be a time when fewer hedges are used in your hedge strategy; instead, look for Fallen Angels that have a solid base for earnings growth combined with a low expectation.

### THE GREAT VOID

Markets don't always move higher or lower. Sometimes they are stagnant and neutral. The Great Void is like a black hole you go in and then get shot out of light-years away (I understand this to be technically incorrect). So much happens, yet you remain the same. Void markets are dangerous because on a real return basis, you could have a minimal return on your investment many years later, which would support my argument that a buy-and-hold strategy is not so rosy. As a matter of fact, if you figure out what the market would have returned to you from, say, 1950 to 1985, or virtually any twenty-five-year period before then, your return would likely not be higher than 6 percent! It only is increased after the 1980s bull market is added in. If we assume another great market is gone for a while, this is the kind of return that will be likely.

After a great bull, the markets will usually retreat into give-back mode. During subsequent years they go about finding themselves again (we all need to find ourselves at some point, right?). So begins the Great Void. To be sure, there will be cyclical bulls, and cyclical bears, but a return to Camelot will most likely take years to realize. As I write this toward the end of 2008, the markets are about where they were eight years ago, when the bull markets ended. Certainly, the markets have rallied, and they have also sold off, but the result is the same—the Great Void.

This period of lack of true direction in the market is nothing new. In fact, many will argue that this is the cycle that U.S. markets will fall into for the next several years.

**Periods of Void**

> March 1937–January 1950 (13 years)
> January 1966–October 1982 (15 years, 9 months)
> January 2000–?

This is a fascinating graph. Eight years of nothing. But here is the important thing to remember—if you had started the "post-bull" graph in October 2000, at the bottom of the bear, you may

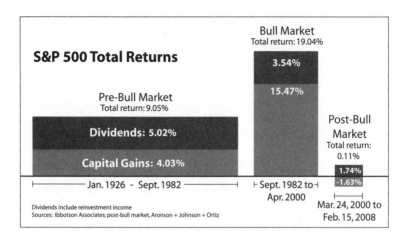

S&P 500 Total Returns

Bull Market
Total return: 19.04%

3.54%

15.47%

Pre-Bull Market
Total return: 9.05%

Dividends: 5.02%

Capital Gains: 4.03%

Post-Bull
Market
Total return:
0.11%

1.74%

-1.63%

Jan. 1926 - Sept. 1982

Sept. 1982 to
Apr. 2000

Mar. 24, 2000 to
Feb. 15, 2008

Dividends include reinvestment income
Sources: Ibbotson Associates; post-bull market, Aronson + Johnson + Ortiz

have doubled your money. But the next downside could wipe out your gains.

In the Great Void, taking two steps forward and two steps backward can be costly. If you take into account inflation, tax, and the time value of money, the effects can be devastating. Don't lose your gains as a market turns bearish! The bear is NOT your friend—it is your prey.

I will say it until I can't: The bear is not your friend. Losses in a bear market wipe away the profits of the bull market. You will think of every reason a falling market isn't a bear market. You'll call it a buying opportunity. You will convince yourself you don't lose until you sell. I'd rather pounce into the market right before the bear goes into hibernation and pounce off late in the bull cycle, and then repeat. The good news is that there are enough bear markets taking place that you can usually find one to buy into (perhaps through a Fallen Angel). Then you can reinvest in an Uncorrelated market. The good news is that money is always in motion; it just changes its address. Somewhere a great trade exists.

### Top 12 Bear Markets

| | |
|---|---|
| 11.21.1916–12.19.1917 | – 40 |
| 11.03.1919–09.24.1921 | – 47 |
| 09.03.1929–11.13.1929 | – 48 |
| 04.17.1930–07.08.1932 | – 86 |
| 09.07.1932–02.27.1933 | – 37 |
| 03.10.1937–03.31.1938 | – 49 |
| 09.12.1939–04.28.1942 | – 40 |
| 12.03.1968–05.26.1970 | – 36 |
| 01.11.1973–12.06.1974 | – 45 |
| 08.25.1987–10.19.1987 | – 36 |
| 01.14.2000–09.21.2001 | – 29 |
| 03.19.2002–10.09.2002 | – 31 |

Arguably many of these seemingly separate bear markets were one long secular bear market. If you go back to a date in 1999, the market went higher (bull), lower (bear), higher again (bull), but through the gyration, we are back to being even. It is interesting to look at the list of top bear markets. In almost every decade at least one significant bear market occurred. The 1990s is one notable exception—something we are paying for today.

Bear markets begin with a 20 percent decline from the previous market's high. Most bear markets don't simply stop after the 20 percent decline and start to move higher; most bear markets see continued selling. The top twelve bear markets chart above supports this fact. Further, it will take most of the year for a bear to run its course. A common mistake is for an investor to run in too soon, thinking that valuation is low, and supporting the "buy low and sell high" argument. Should you buy too early, you forget that P3 includes multiple indicators; valuation is just one component and surely not enough to base a buy on!

Another interesting fact is that the worst bear markets usually led or were concurrent with a recession. We need to understand the direction of the economy (P3). Many of the other, smaller bear markets were simply valuation contractions, and the bear markets worked as an effective self-correcting mechanism. The notable exception to this was in 1987's crash. No recession occurred; the sell-off was primarily one of valuation (and panic), which quickly corrected itself.

### Early Bear Warnings

As a predator, your keen senses should smell a bear a mile away. In the jungle every kill is a bit different from the one before. Every day brings something different: a fire, a bigger predator, a drought, rain. Yet the king of the jungle thrives. Your job is not to look for one specific trigger for each bear market—but to play the odds based on what *trend* is being revealed: not based on your emotions, not based on your intuition, but based on what the indicators state.

### Economy

1. If the bear market is tied to a potential economic slowdown, the market will initiate a sell-off. The sell-off will be viewed, early on, as a buying opportunity by the so-called experts. Don't be so sure. Start tracking the signs of both an economic top, coinciding with valuation, and weakening Investment Psyche/Market Behavior.

2. Although the economic cycle may still be profitable, you are trying to determine if cracks are increasing. Reviewing P3 Economic, you will see a slowdown in manufacturing and in the market (in particular the discretionary sector) and a widening of the credit spread. This means corporate bonds

are paying an interest rate higher than the traditional difference in their rate compared to a Treasury bond of a like term.

3. Also look at areas of the economy that deal with debt and
borrowing. If borrowing is slowing down, it could affect
spending and demand.

## Valuation

1. The market will be well above historical valuations. Stock
prices will grow faster than earnings growth.
2. Due to high valuation, stocks are severely punished when and
if they don't reach inflated earnings expectations provided
by analysts.
3. Look for potentially lower profits due to effects of higher
interest rates over time.
4. Look more at current earnings and sales numbers as opposed to what is projected—if the projection is foolishly
high, the valuation is projected artificially lower than what
will actually transpire. Compare these earnings and sales
numbers to the stock price and determine if the price-to-
sales and price-to-earnings numbers are significantly higher
than the company and sector's long-term average (1.5 times).

## Investor Psychology

1. The ratio of stocks on the NYSE reaching new highs compared with those reaching new lows has recently peaked and
is trending lower.
2. Breadth is starting to deteriorate. Fewer stocks are being actively traded.

3. The mood may still be euphoric, but you can sense the irrational rationalization (the body snatchers have come).

4. Consumer confidence—look at the current consumer confidence reading. Then compare this with the reading six months ago. Economists say that any reading over 90 is "bullish." However, if six months ago the number was much higher and it is trending lower, the salient point is the trend, not the final reading. If the trend is lower by 10 points from where it was six months earlier, this is a sign of a peak.

## What to Do in a Secular Bear

1. For your Core strategy, if you cannot find the companies that meet your criteria, it is acceptable to hold cash. Remember, even in bear markets, the strongest stocks will rise. Stocks with the strongest earnings and sales in relation to their multiples as well as those stocks that have the strongest upside guidance tend to outperform. Also look for higher profit margins and rising dividends. Both are part of the screens that we have already created for you in Rising Stars and Pounce for Income and Growth.

2. Companies that are buying back their stock, paying and increasing dividends, and enjoy low betas outperform in bear markets.*

3. For Best in Show, System 2: Tactical, stay with leadership. Keep a tight three-month monitoring system and forgo any sector that has enjoyed leader status for a rolling eighteen

---

* This data is, in part, supported by a study by James Davis and Anand Desai, both of Kansas State University. The paper is titled "Stock Returns, Beta and Firm Size: The Case of Bull, Bear, and Flat Markets."

months, proceeding to the next leadership candidate. If all P3 indicators are negative, you must refrain from investing until at least two P3 indicators are aggressively undervalued, or two indicators are trending higher.

4. This is a strong time for System 3: Uncorrelated/Hedge. You are seeking negative uncorrelated asset classes, weakest sectors for shorting, and cash. Bear markets are usually not ideal times for Fallen Angels, as weak sectors and stocks usually stay weak in bear markets.

## SUMMARY

Ahh, what a relief it is. You now possess an investment platform. This system is your secret weapon in the fight toward investment greatness. To possess a superior model designed to provide positive alpha and positive returns—*because* of economic adversity—and to do so with the investment strategies you have been given, is nothing short of raw power. Go get some.

# 14

## Pounce into the Future

At this point, assuming you have studied *Pounce*, you are feeling relived and happy. Happy to know that you have more than enough opportunities to feast in any market. Happy to know you don't need to consider every piece of news, rumor, or investment idea that comes across your desk, as it is already incorporated into your P3 indicators. And happy to have a Pounce Platform, and the investment strategies with which to capitalize on your pouncing ability.

So what of the future? You have to know by now that "whatever happens" it is different this time. Whatever curveball is thrown at you, the market, or the future, you are watching this process unfold as if in slow motion. Happy to have a curveball, recession, or bear market thrown at you—it allows you to get your groove on and take advantage of the herd's stupidity.

Think back to Book One. We trained you to create a system—to use all of your evolved predatory instincts, as intuition is simply not good enough for this arena. In fact, you probably have surmised that greatness is realized by being counterintuitive, not intuitive!

## WATER IS THE NEW OIL—AND OTHER PREDICTIONS

The headlines in the future will be dominated by statements such as "Is Water Becoming the 'New Oil'?" (Mark Clayton, *Christian Science Monitor*, May 29, 2008). The article gives many examples of water shortages, including the fact that public fountains are dry in Barcelona, Spain. A tanker docked in Spain carrying five million gallons of water—and the country is lining up more shipments as a result of horrific shortages. Australia's big cash crop, wine, is basically lost due to a multiyear drought.

Will stocks that are affiliated with water rise? Perhaps. I obviously will stick to my three Pounce systems, and if any water companies fit into the Core, Tactical, or Uncorrelated asset classes, I would be free to pounce. But not because of a headline!

Consider water, solar, and agriculture (as they are the possible bubbles forming). I am not sure if the fundamentals would support a purchase. That does not mean that a related pounce couldn't be made. What about the shipping company that is transporting all that water? What about the farm equipment company that is helping make agriculture companies more efficient? This is how you can find possible pounces in every situation.

But perhaps I missed the point of the articles I have been reading about water shortages. Maybe the point is that this could be a serious problem for our world. I obviously do not wish this to be the case, and hope it is not. I will advocate and continue to push our scientists, politicians, and people of the world to advance solutions in an effort to make sure the problem continues to be addressed.

Of course, if the world got to the point that energy, other commodities, and water consumed 75 percent of our expenses, the stock market would probably not fair too well. Actually, our world would not be a very happy place. I should rely on the fact that your Pounce systems will reflect this. Still, using the 20 percent rule, perhaps if the "dire" news did come to fruition (and it is not usually as bad as the headline), these companies would be the leading companies, and you would be poised to pounce.

## A FEW MORE HEADLINES

- According to the World Bank, just over one billion people live on one dollar a day or less.
- According to Goldman Sachs, the cost of ethanol from corn is now more than $80 per barrel.
- In Saudi Arabia, water reserves will last less than 10 years. It is also anticipated the country will import 100% of its food in the near future.

## WHAT CAN ONE EXPECT OF THE STOCK MARKET OVER THE NEXT TEN YEARS?

The question is inevitable and, I guess, fair. Remember, however, I am simply trying to add alpha, so the actual return on the stock market, as a whole, is not as important to me as my personal return. This said, if you study long-term averages, I don't see a "super bull" coming back within the next five years. I base this on the fact that valuation is not cheap, and the world growth rate has slowed a bit. The valuation and slower growth lead me to believe a roller-coaster market will continue for at least three to five years. This is, in fact, the Great Void. I would not be surprised at all if major stock markets are valued, three to five years from now, very close to today's value. If that seems far-fetched, remember that from 2000 until July 2008 (when this book was completed) the Standard & Poor's 500 Index is actually down 2 percent. If you computed the returns using inflation-adjusted numbers, the return would be significantly less. If a horrible depression "killed" the stock market, it would take several years for the Investment Psyche/Market Behavior to turn positive again. So I repeat, it will take several years for a secular bull to arise again.

Maybe, just maybe, the markets might earn 5 percent annualized over the next five years (this may be generous). If you are looking for the calculation, I didn't take a long-term earnings trend and divide it by the price of the market today. It would still be simply a guess. If I did the math that way, the number would be lower.

What that means is that the Pounce investor should thrive. Many cyclical, shorter-term bull and bear markets will occur. Instead of being whipsawed, your monthly meetings will position you to take advantage of the foolishness of investors as they "run with the bulls" and get smacked by the bears.

Should stocks simply move up and down the trendline, and earnings slowly yet steadily increase, valuations will become cheaper. The world will be ready for faster earnings growth and global expansion once again. When this occurs a great bull will emerge.

So we end where we begin. With the foolishness of the herd, and the belief that having a system allows you to master your kingdom and thrive through the chaos.

## WILL GLOBAL MARKETS OFFER A DIFFERENT OUTLOOK?

As you have surmised, I am not an anything "bug." I am not a gold bug, a global bug, a commodity bug, or any bug. All I do is look for the right time to get in and the right time to get off.

Global investing used to be attractive in your System 3: Uncorrelated. These markets did not move in tandem with ours, and could in fact truly act as a hedge. That was then. Now, if you compare various global markets with their U.S. counterparts (small global stocks to small U.S. stocks), you see that the correlation is very high. In fact, the correlation could be higher than 70 percent!

We must analyze each global market as we would any U.S. market—based on the valuation, economy, and Investment Psyche/Market Behavior. It is really that simple.

I love it when people say, "I love the Indian market, or the Chinese market." As we have proved, by the time one of these sectors becomes an obsession among people, the bubble has formed, the easy money has been made, and soon it will be time to get off!

Instead of saying, "I like China," does it not make sense to buy shipbuilders based in the Bahamas (or Greece, or wherever else) that offer a stock with a low valuation, that move products to and from China, capitalizing on the Chinese market? This is opposed to buying directly into China with an incredibly high valuation. If you love Hong Kong, instead of buying a ritually valued Hong Kong market, does it not make sense to look to Fallen Angel global banks to pounce on?

## CAN THE PERSONAL POUNCE PLATFORM
## BE MODIFIED AT ALL?

Absolutely. Your Personal Pounce Platform can and should be modified. As you become more comfortable with your investment strategy and your investment systems, you have many options for modification.

For example, you might add gold and other commodities to

your System 2: Tactical or System 3: Uncorrelated/Hedge. If all P3 readings are bearish, one of the best-performing asset classes is gold. I would then state that although sometimes gold is correlated to the market, it is often uncorrelated. As an investor, I do not understand the value of gold, so it is hard for me to justify getting involved in it. However, as a Pounce investor, you must remember that I do what works. And what works with quite a bit of accuracy is gold during extremely poor periods.

Of late, commodities have been correlated to the markets, but over the long term they have very little correlation. It may make sense to add a commodity index to your Uncorrelated/Hedge asset class. However, you must remember that you will own commodity-based stocks in your Core and Uncorrelated (through pair trading) already.

Some of you may even consider fixed income such as bonds in your Uncorrelated investment system. After all, fixed income often moves in the opposite direction to that of the equity markets. So if you did wish to include bonds, it is only fitting to include them inside of your uncorrelated portion. I kept the Personal Pounce Platform all equity.

## WHAT MORE IS NEEDED?

The Personal Pounce Platform is a terrific investment model. However, as important as it is, it is not, as we briefly discussed in Book One, your wealth plan. It is not your personal Alpha system. The Pounce Platform may be a large percentage of your assets, but it is necessary and prudent to keep enough cash for six to twelve months' worth of expenses. You must be able to take excess cash flow and invest it in the Pounce Platform. You need funds that are "goal-oriented"—for a new home or boat in five years. The Personal Pounce Platform may not provide for this. Perhaps as you need income, you need a higher percentage of your assets in bonds and other investments, both equity and debt, that pay income. These strategies and thoughts are all components of a wealth plan or alpha system that is well thought through. If you don't have one—get one! Contact me, I'll help.

I am absolutely certain of a few things. I am certain that people are going to overreact to the upside and overreact to the downside. I am certain that sensational headlines are going to help fuel these overreactions. I am certain that new technology, globalization, and innovation will continue to fuel this business cycle, setting up a perfect Pouncing opportunity.

# 15

## Pounce Rules

Every day, I am presented with insightful and intelligent questions. These are questions from every angle as it relates to investing, creating a proper investment model, and which theories I subscribe to. I have been keeping a list of these questions, which I would like to address and answer in this chapter.

**Q:** *What do you think is the most surprising fact about the success of the Pounce investment system?*

**A:** I believe intuition and gut reactions adversely affect investment success. Truly great investors follow a system and do not have preconceived notions. Pounce provides an objective, step-by-step process. It is easy to follow. It requires attention only once per month, and all of my testing and implementation suggest that it will continue to thrive in all markets, including chaotic, crazy times.

**Q:** *Do you find any constraints or absolutes as they relate to successful investment strategies?*

**A:** Evaluating a company for a long-term buy-and-hold strategy, or evaluating a company that you would wish to purchase (like a small business), is much different from evaluating a company based on making a winning, relatively short-term investment.

I believe that buy-and-hold investment strategies will be very poor performing strategies over the next several years. I think the best valuation strategy for pinpointing stocks positioned to rise would be to pay attention to earnings expectations and earnings upgrades—they are much more important drivers of a stock's future price than the actual earnings growth. The valuation at which a company trades is important for the long term in forecasting great secular bull and bear markets. However, it is not as important as projected earnings are for short-term cyclical bull and bear markets.

**Q:** *What do you think an investor could hope for in long-term returns from the stock market?*

**A:** I think the typical buy-and-hold investor could hope to earn somewhere in the 6 percent range—depending on the timing of the investment, of course. The market is still expensive, and we have a long way to go to get rid of excesses of the 1990s as well as the credit bubble that burst in 2007.

Take into consideration the fact that from the late 1920s up until the 1982 bull market, stocks earned just about 9 percent. About half of that resulted from dividends. On the other hand, the great bull market that began in 1982 and ended in 2000 enjoyed a return of over 14 percent—mostly as a result of capital gains, not dividends.

If you change your investment platform and learn how to invest actively (using the Pounce Platform, of course), I think a return of somewhere north of 8 percent is achievable.

**Q:** *What do you have to say about the advice to buy-and-hold investments?*

**A:** I believe in buying and holding an investment until my investment strategy tells me to sell. It may be a month after I buy the stock, or a year. I do believe most people hold an investment too long. This often costs them dearly.

**Q:** *What is your take on passive investing and indexes?*

**A:** For the person who has no system, I believe investing in an index is better than haphazard investing. Long-term, the stock market has proven to be the best-performing asset class (compare with bonds and cash). This has been so in most ten-year periods and virtually all fifteen-year periods. It is my steadfast belief that a prudent system can and should be able to beat the index. If there are 500 stocks in the S&P, I'll bet you can train yourself to find the top 100. Further, consider the time period from the beginning of 2000 until the middle of 2008. The Standard & Poor's 500 Index would have delivered a negative return. The Pounce Platform should have delivered quite a positive return.

**Q:** *How much time should one devote to conducting research?*

**A:** I use my three Power Pounce Indicators and the Pounce Platform, and recommend trading once per month. It doesn't take that much time at all. I think you will enjoy the monthly agenda included in Book Three.

**Q:** *Is it your belief that in order to receive higher returns, one has to be exposed to higher risk?*

**A:** First, let's define risk. I do not believe that the average person truly understands this concept. Risk is a quantifiable likelihood of loss, or the possibility of the capital you have earning less than expected. I believe in minimizing risk exposure through prudent adherence to investment strategies, asset allocation, and time.

The old rule states that the higher the risk, the higher the return. Interestingly, studies show investments that are "more conservative" outperform over time. Stocks that are considered lower risk as measured by lower price to sales, price to earnings, and a lower beta outperform, over extended periods of time, their counterparts that have higher ratios.

**Q:** *What are the two most important ingredients to successful investing?*

**A:** The first ingredient is to have a system. I enjoy tracking the investment newsletters that Mark Hulbert of the Hulbert Financial Digest compiles. He has studied this extensively, and the newsletters that are the longest-term winners are the ones that stick to their system and do not deviate, through good or bad. In fact, two of the best performers pounced on the market in two totally different strategies. One bought stocks with big, strong momentum; the other bought deep value. Yet they both outperformed.

The second ingredient is discipline. Stick to your system and invest properly when it is most advantageous so as not to lose money.

Although you asked for two, I have to say the third (everything moves in threes) is to have a great system, like Pounce.

**Q:** *How can someone make money during the upheaval of bubbles and other chaotic markets?*

**A:** Chaotic market environments are ever-present and it is because of these environments that the short-term mispriced opportunities are created. Back to discussing risk. If you had the opportunity to purchase incredible assets at discounts because of recessions or lack of the herd recognizing the opportunity, that's great. Conversely, if you can easily see that the herd has gone in too deep and created a bubble, you can calmly and logically play the downside too.

**Q:** *You talk so calmly and logically about all of this. What is your secret?*

**A:** Read chapter 3, "Animal Instincts." I describe how our brain is already wired in such a way that we are predisposed to fail as investors. I don't mean to pass the buck and say it is not your fault, but you need to know why you make the mistakes you do. Much of it is because your intuition often makes illogical decisions, which may seem logical at the time. For further reading into the fascinating subject of neuroeconomics, numerous research papers and experiments are available. The book Jason Zweig wrote, *Your Money & Your Brain*, is fine work. Go get it.

**Q:** *Is there validity to any of the market-beating ideas that are bandied about?*

**A:** Not really. For every black box system, an exception exists. Look, regardless of the system there is one truth that continues to surface—it is all a bunch of noise. I have no time or patience for noise.

What I have ascertained is that there are three evaluation methods—valuation, economy, and investor psychology. I call these indicators the Power of 3. They work to determine where the market is and where it is possibly going.

From the Power of 3 one can build an Investment Platform—the Personal Pounce Platform. I chose three investment systems for my investment platforms, including:

> System 1—Core
> System 2—Tactical
> System 3—Uncorrelated/Hedge

The bottom line is my life is pretty simple. I have a near-perfect investment platform. I take advantage of all markets, all chaotic period, all bulls, and have a great time doing so.

**Q:** *How do you feel about market timing?*

**A:** I enjoy it when you hear someone expound on the virtues of one strategy or another, but I do not believe in market timing per se. That said, if gross anomalies exist, on the upside or the downside— I will be investing accordingly.

Many studies have been performed to include investor returns by timing their mutual fund purchases, or individual stocks, and even markets. Most of these studies conclude that a buy-and-hold strategy over the long run outperforms the timing strategies. I do not argue with these studies. What I do think is that, based on my three powerful strategies for determining market direction, I will alter my Pounce Platform accordingly. I will not sit by, fully long invested (without cash or hedges), and watch a bear market wipe me out.

**Q:** *Whom does* Pounce *appeal to? What do you hope to accomplish by writing this book?*

**A:** I think virtually anyone with intellectual curiosity can benefit and learn from the strategies introduced in *Pounce*. It is thought-provoking, not just a fun fluff read. We go beyond fluff.

I think the analyst who loves data and charts could possibly have a hard time with Pounce. They will be looking for more data to compute, and more systems to test. This is the antithesis of Pounce. The whole theory behind Pounce is to add alpha and provide an absolute return. Alpha, meaning to help you make more money than the return the markets would deliver. And an absolute return is to enjoy consistent positive returns—to enjoy these returns not in spite of the chaotic markets but because of them.

Lots of books teach you how to analyze the fundamentals of a company. I don't know how that relates to making money, great investing, or wealth accumulation. *Pounce* was intended to be a research book, with plenty of charts and graphs. That would not be something I believe in. Remember, I am trying to demonstrate to the academic that he is thinking too much!

*Pounce* is a book for everyone. I think most people will enjoy a book that is focused on both education and effective strategies.

**Q:** *Are you concerned about the value of the dollar, the credit crunch, the cost of crude oil, and the effects that these issues can have on the market?*

**A:** No. Read the book, and you will realize how these are all pouncing opportunities. For example, if concerns about inflation abound, chances are interest rates would head higher. Many people perceive this as a negative for the stock market, but it is not necessarily a negative. Perhaps the stock market will sell off on this news, giving the true investment predator a window of opportunity in which to Pounce.

**Q:** *Is it true that small-cap value tends to be the best long-term performer? Should investors overweight their portfolios with this asset class?*

**A:** Every sector of the market and every market based on size will ebb and flow. In fact, one of the few truths to investing is that everything reverts to the mean, eventually. There will always be a reversion to the mean. The leadership sectors will become fully valued and underperform against the new leadership sectors. Your job as an investor is to catch the Rising Star, get out before it becomes a Shooting Star, and then consider buying it back when it becomes a Fallen Angel. I don't worry as to what is the "right" sector for the time. My investment strategies and screens tell me what is right.

**Q:** *How easy is it to maintain my own Personal Pounce Platform?*

**A:** It's so easy, you will only have to do it once a month. You actually will do some research heading into your Pounce Platform Meeting, but you will only make changes once per month.

# ACKNOWLEDGMENTS

This book was a huge, combined effort. Many people deserve recognition.

First, the entire team at Ken Stern & Associates who contributed, were critical of, challenged, and propelled me. In particular, Anish Ramachandran is a wizard with anything analytical. Eric Hoffman is so smart, no matter the task, he knows how to get there quickest. Kelly Kurtz's early edits, thoughts, and love for graphs (I am running as I say this) helped craft the manuscript.

My agent, who believed in the project and always took my calls (I kept using different phone numbers so he didn't know who was calling). Thank you, Jeremy Katz, of Sanford J. Greenburger and Associates.

Phil Revzin, senior editor at St. Martin's Press. Phil, your pinpoint accuracy, guidance, and belief in the project took *Pounce* from good to great.

Stacey, for your contributions, for keeping me organized, for guiding me. I truly understand what it is meant to have a friend and advisor who truly wishes the success. Now, on to the next project! ☺

Finally, to Rachael and Ella. You girls, as always, were and are wonderful. Your patience, understanding, and curiosity are my never-ending source of pride and joy. I will never forget our flight back from Tennessee (all five stops!). At one point, I'm trying to bang out a chapter, you both are playing with me, a baby is crying in front of us, and I almost snap. You both sensed this, shielded me, soothed me, told me to take a breath and focus (this after both of you had been up half the night), and then played wonderfully together, allowing me to memorialize, within these pages, whatever thought I felt so urgently about.

# INDEX

# ABOUT THE AUTHOR

Ken Stern is the author of six top-selling personal finance/ retirement books including: *Secrets of the Investment All-Stars*; *Senior Savvy*; *50 Fabulous Places to Retire in America*; *Safeguard Your Hard-Earned Savings*; *The Comprehensive Guide to Social Security and Medicare*; and *To Hell and Back.*

An accomplished speaker, he has appeared on such national shows as *Today*, *CNBC Money Talk*, *Power Lunch*, *MarketWatch*, and CNN. They have called upon Mr. Stern for his advice regarding the financial markets. In a letter to Mr. Stern, Katie Couric, then of NBC's *Today* stated: "Information like this will come in handy sooner than I realized." He has been quoted in several periodicals including *Fortune*, *New York Times*, and *Miami Herald.*

As host of the popular *Asset Planning University* radio show on San Diego's KOGO 600 AM and Chicago's *Newstalk* WIND 560 AM, Mr. Stern is able to provide listeners with complicated financial information in an easy-to-understand format. He has been a guest on literally hundreds of radio shows nationwide and is a regular guest on the *Money in the Morning* show with George Chamberlin, also heard on KOGO 600 AM.

Mr. Stern is president and founder of Asset Planning Solutions, Inc., and Ken Stern & Associates, provider of professionally managed portfolio services. Mr. Stern has received a coveted spot in the Bloomberg Wealth Manager annual ranking of America's top wealth managers since 2004.

He has earned the title of Certified Financial Planner from the College of Financial Planning™ in Denver, Colorado.

Originally from Farmington Hills, Michigan, Mr. Stern enjoys traveling, skiing, public speaking, writing, and reading.